DEPARTMENT OF JUSTICE REPORT REGARDING THE CRIMINAL INVESTIGATION INTO THE SHOOTING DEATH OF MICHAEL BROWN BY FERGUSON, MISSOURI POLICE OFFICER DARREN WILSON

MARCH 4, 2015

Table of Contents

I.   Introduction

At approximately noon on Saturday, August 9, 2014, Officer Darren Wilson of the Ferguson Police Department ("FPD") shot and killed Michael Brown, an unarmed 18-year-old. The Criminal Section of the Department of Justice Civil Rights Division, the United States Attorney's Office for the Eastern District of Missouri, and the Federal Bureau of Investigation ("FBI") (collectively, "The Department") subsequently opened a criminal investigation into whether the shooting violated federal law. The Department has determined that the evidence does not support charging a violation of federal law. This memorandum details the Department's investigation, findings, and conclusions. Part I provides an introduction and overview. Part II summarizes the federal investigation and the evidence uncovered during the course of the investigation, and discusses the applicable federal criminal civil rights law and standards of federal prosecution. Part III provides a more in-depth summary of the evidence. Finally, Part IV provides a detailed legal analysis of the evidence and explains why the evidence does not support an indictment of Darren Wilson.

The Department conducted an extensive investigation into the shooting of Michael Brown. Federal authorities reviewed physical, ballistic, forensic, and crime scene evidence; medical reports and autopsy reports, including an independent autopsy performed by the United States Department of Defense Armed Forces Medical Examiner Service ("AFMES"); Wilson's personnel records; audio and video recordings; and internet postings. FBI agents, St. Louis County Police Department ("SLCPD") detectives, and federal prosecutors and prosecutors from the St. Louis County Prosecutor's Office ("county prosecutors") worked cooperatively to both independently and jointly interview more than 100 purported eyewitnesses and other individuals claiming to have relevant information. SLCPD detectives conducted an initial canvass of the area on the day of the shooting. FBI agents then independently canvassed more than 300 residences to locate and interview additional witnesses. Federal and local authorities collected cellular phone data, searched social media sites, and tracked down dozens of leads from community members and dedicated law enforcement email addresses and tip lines in an effort to investigate every possible source of information.

The principles of federal prosecution, set forth in the United States Attorneys' Manual ("USAM"), require federal prosecutors to meet two standards in order to seek an indictment. First, we must be convinced that the potential defendant committed a federal crime. *See* USAM § 9-27.220 (a federal prosecution should be commenced only when an attorney for the government "believes that the person's conduct constitutes a federal offense"). Second, we must also conclude that we would be likely to prevail at trial, where we must prove the charges beyond a reasonable doubt. *See* USAM § 9-27.220 (a federal prosecution should be commenced only when "the admissible evidence will probably be sufficient to sustain a conviction"); Fed R. Crim P. 29(a)(prosecution must present evidence sufficient to sustain a conviction). Taken together, these standards require the Department to be convinced both that a federal crime occurred and that it can be proven beyond a reasonable doubt at trial.[1]

In order to make the proper assessment under these standards, federal prosecutors evaluated physical, forensic, and potential testimonial evidence in the form of witness accounts. As detailed below, the physical and forensic evidence provided federal prosecutors with a benchmark against which to measure the credibility of each witness account, including that of Darren Wilson. We compared individual witness accounts to the physical and forensic evidence, to other credible witness accounts, and to each witness's own prior statements made throughout the investigations, including the proceedings before the St. Louis County grand jury ("county grand jury"). We worked with federal and local law enforcement officers to interview witnesses, to include re-interviewing certain witnesses in an effort to evaluate inconsistencies in their accounts and to obtain more detailed information. In so doing, we assessed the witnesses' demeanor, tone, bias, and ability to accurately perceive or recall the events of August 9, 2014. We credited and determined that a jury would appropriately credit those witnesses whose accounts were consistent with the physical evidence and consistent with other credible witness accounts. In the case of witnesses who made multiple statements, we compared those statements to determine whether they were materially consistent with each other and considered the timing and circumstances under which the witnesses gave the statements. We did not credit and determined that a jury appropriately would not credit those witness accounts that were contrary to the physical and forensic evidence, significantly inconsistent with other credible witness accounts, or significantly inconsistent with that witness's own prior statements.

Based on this investigation, the Department has concluded that Darren Wilson's actions do not constitute prosecutable violations under the applicable federal criminal civil rights statute, 18 U.S.C. § 242, which prohibits uses of deadly force that are "objectively unreasonable," as defined by the United States Supreme Court. The evidence, when viewed as a whole, does not support the conclusion that Wilson's uses of deadly force were "objectively unreasonable" under the Supreme Court's definition. Accordingly, under the governing federal law and relevant standards set forth in the USAM, it is not appropriate to present this matter to a federal grand jury for indictment, and it should therefore be closed without prosecution.

II. Summary of the Evidence, Investigation, and Applicable Law

A. Summary of the Evidence

Within two minutes of Wilson's initial encounter with Brown on August 9, 2014, FPD officers responded to the scene of the shooting, and subsequently turned the matter over to the SLCPD for investigation. SLCPD detectives immediately began securing and processing the scene and conducting initial witness interviews. The FBI opened a federal criminal civil rights investigation on August 11, 2014. Thereafter, federal and county authorities conducted cooperative, yet independent investigations into the shooting of Michael Brown.

---

[1] The threshold determination that a case meets the standard for indictment rests with the prosecutor, *Wayte v. United States*, 470 U.S. 598, 607 (1985), and is "one of the most considered decisions a federal prosecutor makes." USAM 9-27.200, Annotation.

The encounter between Wilson and Brown took place over an approximately two-minute period of time at about noon on August 9, 2014. Wilson was on duty and driving his department-issued Chevy Tahoe SUV westbound on Canfield Drive in Ferguson, Missouri when he saw Brown and his friend, Witness 101,[2] walking eastbound in the middle of the street. Brown and Witness 101 had just come from Ferguson Market and Liquor ("Ferguson Market"), a nearby convenience store, where, at approximately 11:53 a.m., Brown stole several packages of cigarillos. As captured on the store's surveillance video, when the store clerk tried to stop Brown, Brown used his physical size to stand over him and forcefully shove him away. As a result, an FPD dispatch call went out over the police radio for a "stealing in progress." The dispatch recordings and Wilson's radio transmissions establish that Wilson was aware of the theft and had a description of the suspects as he encountered Brown and Witness 101.

As Wilson drove toward Brown and Witness 101, he told the two men to walk on the sidewalk. According to Wilson's statement to prosecutors and investigators, he suspected that Brown and Witness 101 were involved in the incident at Ferguson Market based on the descriptions he heard on the radio and the cigarillos in Brown's hands. Wilson then called for backup, stating, "Put me on Canfield with two and send me another car." Wilson backed up his SUV and parked at an angle, blocking most of both lanes of traffic, and stopping Brown and Witness 101 from walking any further. Wilson attempted to open the driver's door of the SUV to exit his vehicle, but as he swung it open, the door came into contact with Brown's body and either rebounded closed or Brown pushed it closed.

Wilson and other witnesses stated that Brown then reached into the SUV through the open driver's window and punched and grabbed Wilson. This is corroborated by bruising on Wilson's jaw and scratches on his neck, the presence of Brown's DNA on Wilson's collar, shirt, and pants, and Wilson's DNA on Brown's palm. While there are other individuals who stated that Wilson reached out of the SUV and grabbed Brown by the neck, prosecutors could not credit their accounts because they were inconsistent with physical and forensic evidence, as detailed throughout this report.

Wilson told prosecutors and investigators that he responded to Brown reaching into the SUV and punching him by withdrawing his gun because he could not access less lethal weapons while seated inside the SUV. Brown then grabbed the weapon and struggled with Wilson to gain control of it. Wilson fired, striking Brown in the hand. Autopsy results and bullet trajectory, skin from Brown's palm on the outside of the SUV door as well as Brown's DNA on the inside of the driver's door corroborate Wilson's account that during the struggle, Brown used his right hand to grab and attempt to control Wilson's gun. According to three autopsies, Brown sustained a close range gunshot wound to the fleshy portion of his right hand at the base of his right thumb. Soot from the muzzle of the gun found embedded in the tissue of this wound coupled with indicia of thermal change from the heat of the muzzle indicate that Brown's hand was within inches of the muzzle of Wilson's gun when it was fired. The location of the recovered bullet in the side panel of the driver's door, just above Wilson's lap, also corroborates Wilson's account of the struggle over the gun and when the gun was fired, as do witness accounts that Wilson fired at least one shot from inside the SUV.

---

[2] With the exception of Darren Wilson and Michael Brown, the names of individuals have been redacted as a safeguard against an invasion of their personal privacy.

Although no eyewitnesses directly corroborate Wilson's account of Brown's attempt to gain control of the gun, there is no credible evidence to disprove Wilson's account of what occurred inside the SUV. Some witnesses claim that Brown's arms were never inside the SUV. However, as discussed later in this report, those witness accounts could not be relied upon in a prosecution because credible witness accounts and physical and forensic evidence, *i.e.* Brown's DNA inside the SUV and on Wilson's shirt collar and the bullet trajectory and close-range gunshot wound to Brown's hand, establish that Brown's arms and/or torso were inside the SUV.

After the initial shooting inside the SUV, the evidence establishes that Brown ran eastbound on Canfield Drive and Wilson chased after him. The autopsy results confirm that Wilson did not shoot Brown in the back as he was running away because there were no entrance wounds to Brown's back. The autopsy results alone do not indicate the direction Brown was facing when he received two wounds to his right arm, given the mobility of the arm. However, as detailed later in this report, there are no witness accounts that could be relied upon in a prosecution to prove that Wilson shot at Brown as he was running away. Witnesses who say so cannot be relied upon in a prosecution because they have given accounts that are inconsistent with the physical and forensic evidence or are significantly inconsistent with their own prior statements made throughout the investigation.

Brown ran at least 180 feet away from the SUV, as verified by the location of bloodstains on the roadway, which DNA analysis confirms was Brown's blood. Brown then turned around and came back toward Wilson, falling to his death approximately 21.6 feet west of the blood in the roadway. Those witness accounts stating that Brown never moved back toward Wilson could not be relied upon in a prosecution because their accounts cannot be reconciled with the DNA bloodstain evidence and other credible witness accounts.

As detailed throughout this report, several witnesses stated that Brown appeared to pose a physical threat to Wilson as he moved toward Wilson. According to these witnesses, who are corroborated by blood evidence in the roadway, as Brown continued to move toward Wilson, Wilson fired at Brown in what appeared to be self-defense and stopped firing once Brown fell to the ground. Wilson stated that he feared Brown would again assault him because of Brown's conduct at the SUV and because as Brown moved toward him, Wilson saw Brown reach his right hand under his t-shirt into what appeared to be his waistband. There is no evidence upon which prosecutors can rely to disprove Wilson's stated subjective belief that he feared for his safety.

Ballistics analysis indicates that Wilson fired a total of 12 shots, two from the SUV and ten on the roadway. Witness accounts and an audio recording indicate that when Wilson and Brown were on the roadway, Wilson fired three gunshot volleys, pausing in between each one. According to the autopsy results, Wilson shot and hit Brown as few as six or as many as eight times, including the gunshot to Brown's hand. Brown fell to the ground dead as a result of a gunshot to the apex of his head. With the exception of the first shot to Brown's hand, all of the shots that struck Brown were fired from a distance of more than two feet. As documented by crime scene photographs, Brown fell to the ground with his left, uninjured hand balled up by his waistband, and his right, injured hand palm up by his side. Witness accounts and cellular phone video prove that Wilson did not touch Brown's body after he fired the final shot and Brown fell to the ground.

Although there are several individuals who have stated that Brown held his hands up in an unambiguous sign of surrender prior to Wilson shooting him dead, their accounts do not support a prosecution of Wilson. As detailed throughout this report, some of those accounts are inaccurate because they are inconsistent with the physical and forensic evidence; some of those accounts are materially inconsistent with that witness's own prior statements with no explanation, credible for otherwise, as to why those accounts changed over time. Certain other witnesses who originally stated Brown had his hands up in surrender recanted their original accounts, admitting that they did not witness the shooting or parts of it, despite what they initially reported either to federal or local law enforcement or to the media. Prosecutors did not rely on those accounts when making a prosecutive decision.

While credible witnesses gave varying accounts of exactly what Brown was doing with his hands as he moved toward Wilson – *i.e.*, balling them, holding them out, or pulling up his pants up – and varying accounts of how he was moving – *i.e.*, "charging," moving in "slow motion," or "running" – they all establish that Brown was moving toward Wilson when Wilson shot him. Although some witnesses state that Brown held his hands up at shoulder level with his palms facing outward for a brief moment, these same witnesses describe Brown then dropping his hands and "charging" at Wilson.

B. Initial Law Enforcement Investigation

Wilson shot Brown at about 12:02 p.m. on August 9, 2014. Within minutes, FPD officers responded to the scene, as they were already en route from Wilson's initial radio call for assistance. Also within minutes, residents began pouring onto the street. At 12:08 p.m., FPD officers requested assistance from nearby SLCPD precincts. By 12:14 p.m., some members of the growing crowd became increasingly hostile in response to chants of "[We] need to kill these motherfuckers," referring to the police officers on scene. At around the same time, about 12:15 p.m., Witness 147, an FPD sergeant, informed the FPD Chief that there had been a fatal officer-involved shooting. At about 12:23 p.m., after speaking with one of his captains, the FPD Chief contacted the SLCPD Chief and turned over the homicide investigation to the SLCPD. Within twenty minutes of Brown's death, paramedics covered Brown's body with several white sheets.

The SLCPD Division of Criminal Investigation, Bureau of Crimes Against Persons ("CAP") was notified at 12:43 p.m. to report to the crime scene to begin a homicide investigation. When they received notification, SLCPD CAP detectives were investigating an armed, masked hostage situation in the hospice wing at St. Anthony's Medical Center in the south part of St. Louis County, nearly 37 minutes from Canfield Drive. They arrived at Canfield Drive at approximately 1:30 p.m. During that time frame, between about 12:45 p.m. and 1:17 p.m., SLCPD reported gunfire in the area, putting both civilians and officers in danger. As a result, canine officers and additional patrol officers responded to assist with crowd control. SLCPD expanded the perimeter of the crime scene to move the crowd away from Brown's body in an effort to preserve the crime scene for processing.

Upon their arrival, SLCPD detectives from the Bureau of Criminal Identification Crime Scene Unit erected orange privacy screens around Brown's body, and CAP detectives alerted the

St. Louis County Medical Examiner ("SCLME") to respond to the scene. To further protect the integrity of the crime scene, and in accordance with common police practice, SLCPD personnel did not permit family members and concerned neighbors into the crime scene (with one brief exception). Also in accordance with common police practice, crime scene detectives processed the crime scene with Brown's body present. According to SLCPD CAP detectives, they have one opportunity to thoroughly investigate a crime scene before it is forever changed upon the removal of the decedent's body. Processing a homicide scene with the decedent's body present allows detectives, for example, to accurately measure distances, precisely document body position, and note injury and other markings relative to other aspects of the crime scene that photographs may not capture.

In this case, crime scene detectives had to stop processing the scene as a result of two more reports of what sounded like automatic weapons gunfire in the area at 1:55 p.m. and 2:11 p.m., as well as some individuals in the crowd encroaching on the crime scene and chanting, "Kill the Police," as documented by cell phone video. At each of those times, having exhausted their existing resources, SLCPD personnel called emergency codes for additional patrol officers from throughout St. Louis County in increments of twenty-five. Livery drivers sent to transport Brown's body upon completion of processing arrived at 2:20 p.m. Their customary practice is to wait on scene until the body is ready for transport. However, an SLCPD sergeant briefly stopped them from getting out of their vehicle until the gunfire abated and it was safe for them to do so. The SLCME medicolegal investigator arrived at 2:30 p.m. and began conducting his investigation when it was reasonably safe to do so. Detectives were at the crime scene for approximately five and a half hours, and throughout that time, SLCPD personnel continued to seek additional assistance, calling in the Highway Safety Unit at 2:38 p.m. and the Tactical Operations Unit at 2:44 p.m. Witnesses and detectives described the scene as volatile, causing concern for both their personal safety and the integrity of the crime scene. Crime scene detectives and the SLCME medicolegal investigator completed the processing of Brown's body at approximately 4:00 p.m, at which time Brown's body was transported to the Office of the SLCME.

C. Legal Summary

1. The Law Governing Uses of Deadly Force by a Law Enforcement Officer

The federal criminal statute that enforces Constitutional limits on uses of force by law enforcement officers is 18 U.S.C. § 242, which provides in relevant part, as follows:

> Whoever, under color of any law, . . . willfully subjects any person . . . to the deprivation of any rights, privileges, or immunities secured or protected by the Constitution or laws of the United States [shall be guilty of a crime].

To prove a violation of Section 242, the government must prove the following elements beyond a reasonable doubt: (1) that the defendant was acting under color of law, (2) that he deprived a victim of a right protected by the Constitution or laws of the United States, (3) that he acted willfully, and (4) that the deprivation resulted in bodily injury and/or death. There is no dispute that Wilson, who was on duty and working as a patrol officer for the FPD, acted under color of law when he shot Brown, or that the shots resulted in Brown's death. The determination of whether criminal prosecution is appropriate rests on whether there is sufficient evidence to establish that any of the shots fired by Wilson were unreasonable, as defined under federal law, given the facts known to Wilson at the time, and if so, whether Wilson fired the shots with the requisite "willful" criminal intent.

i. *The Shootings Were Not Objectively Unreasonable Uses of Force Under 18 U.S.C. § 242*

In this case, the Constitutional right at issue is the Fourth Amendment's prohibition against unreasonable seizures, which encompasses the right of an arrestee to be free from "objectively unreasonable" force. *Graham v. Connor*, 490 U.S. 386, 396-97 (1989). "The 'reasonableness' of a particular use of force must be judged from the perspective of a reasonable officer on the scene, rather than with the 20/20 vision of hindsight." *Id*. at 396. "Careful attention" must be paid "to the facts and circumstances of each particular case, including the severity of the crime at issue, whether the suspect poses an immediate threat to the safety of the officers or others, and whether he is actively resisting arrest or attempting to evade arrest by flight." *Id*. Allowance must be made for the fact that law enforcement officials are often forced to make split-second judgments in circumstances that are tense, uncertain, and rapidly evolving. *Id*. at 396-97.

The use of deadly force is justified when the officer has "probable cause to believe that the suspect pose[s] a threat of serious physical harm, either to the officer or to others." *Tennessee v. Garner*, 471 U.S. 1, 11 (1985); *see Nelson v. County of Wright*, 162 F.3d 986, 990 (8th Cir. 1998); *O'Bert v. Vargo*, 331 F.3d 29, 36 (2d Cir. 2003) (same as *Garner*); *Deluna v. City of Rockford*, 447 F.3d 1008, 1010 (7th Cir. 2006), *citing Scott v. Edinburg*, 346 F.3d 752, 756 (7th Cir. 2003) (deadly force can be reasonably employed where an officer believes that the suspect's actions place him, or others in the immediate vicinity, in imminent danger of death or serious bodily injury).

As detailed throughout this report, the evidence does not establish that the shots fired by Wilson were objectively unreasonable under federal law. The physical evidence establishes that Wilson shot Brown once in the hand, at close range, while Wilson sat in his police SUV, struggling with Brown for control of Wilson's gun. Wilson then shot Brown several more times from a distance of at least two feet after Brown ran away from Wilson and then turned and faced him. There are no witness accounts that federal prosecutors, and likewise a jury, would credit to support the conclusion that Wilson fired at Brown from behind. With the exception of the two wounds to Brown's right arm, which indicate neither bullet trajectory nor the direction in which Brown was moving when he was struck, the medical examiners' reports are in agreement that the entry wounds from the latter gunshots were to the front of Brown's body, establishing that Brown was facing Wilson when these shots were fired. This includes the fatal shot to the top of Brown's head. The physical evidence also establishes that Brown moved forward toward Wilson after he turned around to face him. The physical evidence is corroborated by multiple eyewitnesses.

Applying the well-established controlling legal authority, including binding precedent from the United States Supreme Court and Eighth Circuit Court of Appeals, the evidence does not establish that it was unreasonable for Wilson to perceive Brown as a threat while Brown was punching and grabbing him in the SUV and attempting to take his gun. Thereafter, when Brown started to flee, Wilson was aware that Brown had attempted to take his gun and suspected that Brown might have been part of a theft a few minutes before. Under the law, it was not unreasonable for Wilson to perceive that Brown posed a threat of serious physical harm, either to him or to others. When Brown turned around and moved toward Wilson, the applicable law and evidence do not support finding that Wilson was unreasonable in his fear that Brown would once again attempt to harm him and gain control of his gun. There are no credible witness accounts that state that Brown was clearly attempting to surrender when Wilson shot him. As detailed throughout this report, those witnesses who say so have given accounts that could not be relied upon in a prosecution because they are irreconcilable with the physical evidence, inconsistent with the credible accounts of other eyewitnesses, inconsistent with the witness's own prior statements, or in some instances, because the witnesses have acknowledged that their initial accounts were untrue.

ii. Wilson Did Not Willfully Violate Brown's Constitutional Right to Be Free from Unreasonable Force

Federal law requires that the government must also prove that the officer acted willfully, that is, "for the specific purpose of violating the law." *Screws v. United States*, 325 U.S. 91, 101-107 (1945) (discussing willfulness element of 18 U.S.C. § 242). The Supreme Court has held that an act is done willfully if it was "committed" either "in open defiance or in reckless disregard of a constitutional requirement which has been made specific or definite." *Screws*, 325 U.S. at 105. The government need not show that the defendant knew a federal statute or law protected the right with which he intended to interfere. *Id.* at 106-07 ("[t]he fact that the defendants may not have been thinking in constitutional terms is not material where their aim was not to enforce local law but to deprive a citizen of a right and that right was protected"); *United States v. Walsh*, 194 F.3d 37, 52-53 (2d Cir. 1999) (holding that jury did not have to find defendant knew of the particular Constitutional provision at issue but that it had to find intent to invade interest protected by Constitution). However, we must prove that the defendant intended to engage in the conduct that violated the Constitution and that he did so knowing that it was a wrongful act. *Id.*

"[A]ll the attendant circumstances" should be considered in determining whether an act was done willfully. *Screws*, 325 U.S. at 107. Evidence regarding the egregiousness of the conduct, its character and duration, the weapons employed and the provocation, if any, is therefore relevant to this inquiry. *Id.* Willfulness may be inferred from blatantly wrongful conduct. *See id.* at 106; *see also United States v. Reese*, 2 F.3d 870, 881 (9th Cir. 1993) ("Intentionally wrongful conduct, because it contravenes a right definitely established in law, evidences a reckless disregard for that right; such reckless disregard, in turn, is the legal equivalent of willfulness."); *United States v. Dise*, 763 F.2d 586, 592 (3d Cir. 1985) (holding that when defendant "invades personal liberty of another, knowing that invasion is violation of state law, [defendant] has demonstrated bad faith and reckless disregard for [federal] constitutional rights"). Mistake, fear, misperception, or even poor judgment does not constitute willful conduct prosecutable under the statute. *See United States v. McClean*, 528 F.2d 1250, 1255 (2d Cir. 1976) (inadvertence or mistake negates willfulness for purposes of 18 U.S.C. § 242).

As detailed below, Wilson has stated his intent in shooting Brown was in response to a perceived deadly threat. The only possible basis for prosecuting Wilson under 18 U.S.C. § 242 would therefore be if the government could prove that his account is not true – *i.e.*, that Brown never punched and grabbed Wilson at the SUV, never attempted to gain control of Wilson's gun, and thereafter clearly surrendered in a way that no reasonable officer could have failed to perceive. There is no credible evidence to refute Wilson's stated subjective belief that he was acting in self-defense. As discussed throughout this report, Wilson's account is corroborated by physical evidence and his perception of a threat posed by Brown is corroborated by other credible eyewitness accounts. Even if Wilson was mistaken in his interpretation of Brown's conduct, the fact that others interpreted that conduct the same way as Wilson precludes a determination that he acted for the purpose of violating the law.

III. Summary of the Evidence

As detailed below, Darren Wilson has stated that he shot Michael Brown in response to a perceived deadly threat. This section begins with Wilson's account because the evidence that follows, in the form of forensic and physical evidence and witness accounts, must disprove his account beyond a reasonable doubt in order for the government to prosecute Wilson.

A. Darren Wilson's Account

Darren Wilson made five voluntary statements following the shooting. Wilson's first statement was to Witness 147, his supervising sergeant at the FPD, who responded to Canfield Drive within minutes and immediately spoke to Wilson.[3] Wilson's second statement was made to an SLCPD detective about 90 minutes later, after Wilson returned to the FPD. This interview continued at a local hospital while Wilson was receiving medical treatment. Third, SLCPD detectives conducted a more thorough interview the following morning, on August 10, 2014. Fourth, federal prosecutors and FBI agents interviewed Wilson on August 22, 2014. Wilson's attorney was present for both interviews with the SLCPD detectives. Two attorneys were present for his interview with federal agents and prosecutors. Wilson's fifth statement occurred when he appeared before the county grand jury for approximately 90 minutes on September 16, 2014.

According to Wilson, he was traveling westbound on Canfield Drive, having just finished another call, when he saw Brown and Witness 101 walking single file in the middle of the street on the yellow line. Wilson had never before met either Brown or Witness 101. Wilson approached Witness 101 first and told him to use the sidewalk because there had been cars trying to pass them. When pressed by federal prosecutors, Wilson denied using profane language, explaining that he was on his way to meet his fiancée for lunch, and did not want to antagonize the two subjects. Witness 101 responded to Wilson that he was almost to his destination, and Wilson replied, "What's wrong with the sidewalk?" Wilson stated that Brown unexpectedly

---

[3] Witness 147 was jointly interviewed by SLCPD detectives and federal agents and prosecutors on August 19, 2014. He then testified before the county grand jury on September 16, 2014. Witness 147 never documented what Wilson told him during those initial few minutes after the shooting. Witness 147 acknowledged that while talking to Wilson, he was also focused on the shooting scene and crowd safety.

responded, "Fuck what you have to say." As Wilson drove past Brown, he saw cigarillos in Brown's hand, which alerted him to a radio dispatch of a "stealing in progress" that he heard a few minutes prior while finishing his last call. Wilson then checked his rearview mirror, and realized that Witness 101 matched the description of the other subject on the radio dispatch.

Wilson requested assistance over the radio, stating that he had two subjects on Canfield Drive. Wilson explained that he intended to stop Brown and Witness 101 and wait for backup before he did any further investigation into the theft. Wilson reversed his vehicle and parked in a manner to block Brown and Witness 101 from walking any further. Upon doing so, he attempted to open his driver's door, and said, "Hey, come here." Before Wilson got his leg out, Brown responded, "What the fuck are you gonna do?"[4] Brown then slammed the door shut and Wilson told him to "get back." Wilson attempted to open the door again. Wilson told the county grand jury that he then told Brown, "Get the fuck back," but Brown did not comply and, using his body, pushed the door closed on Wilson.

Brown placed his hands on the window frame of the driver's door, and again Wilson told Brown to "get back." To Wilson's surprise, Brown then leaned into the driver's window, so that his arms and upper torso were inside the SUV. Brown started assaulting Wilson, "swinging wildly." Brown, still with cigarillos in his hand, turned around and handed the items to Witness 101 using his left hand, telling Witness 101 "take these." Wilson used the opportunity to grab Brown's right arm, but Brown used his left hand to twice punch Wilson's jaw. As Brown assaulted Wilson, Wilson leaned back, blocking the blows with his forearms. Brown hit Wilson on the side of his face and grabbed his shirt, hands, and arms. Wilson feared that Brown's blows could potentially render him unconscious, leaving him vulnerable to additional harm.

Wilson explained that he resorted to his training and the "use of force triangle" to determine how to properly defend himself. Wilson explained that he did not carry a taser, and therefore, his options were mace, his flashlight, his retractable asp baton, and his firearm. Wilson's mace was on his left hip and Wilson explained that he knew that the space within the SUV was too small to use it without incapacitating himself in the process. Wilson's asp baton was located on the back of his duty belt. Wilson determined that not only would he have to lean forward to reach it, giving more of an advantage to Brown, but there was not enough space in the SUV to expand the baton. Wilson's flashlight was in his duty bag on the passenger seat, out of his reach. Wilson explained that his gun, located on his right hip, was his only readily accessible option.

Consequently, while the assault was in progress and Brown was leaning in through the window with his arms, torso, and head inside the SUV, Wilson withdrew his gun and pointed it at Brown. Wilson warned Brown to stop or he was going to shoot him. Brown stated, "You are

---

[4] The Ferguson Market store clerk's daughter stated that Brown used a similar statement when her father tried to stop Brown from stealing cigarillos, i.e., "What you gonna do?" While it might seem odd that a person in Brown's position would verbally confront a police officer, the fact that another witness at a separate location described Brown as speaking similarly a few minutes earlier tends to corroborate Wilson.

too much of a pussy to shoot,"[5] and put his right hand[6] over Wilson's right hand, gaining control of the gun. Brown then maneuvered the gun so that it was pointed down at Wilson's left hip. Wilson explained that Brown's size and strength, coupled with his standing position outside the SUV relative to Wilson's seated position inside the SUV, rendered Wilson completely vulnerable. Wilson stated that he feared Brown was going to shoot him because Brown had control of the gun. Wilson managed to use his left elbow to brace against the seat, gaining enough leverage to push the gun forward until it lined up with the driver's door, just under the handle. Wilson explained that he twice pulled the trigger but the gun did not fire, most likely because Brown's hand was preventing the gun from functioning properly. Wilson pulled the trigger a third time and the gun fired into the door. Immediately, glass shattered because the window had been down, and Wilson noticed blood on his own hand. Wilson initially thought he had been cut by the glass.

Brown appeared to be momentarily startled because he briefly backed up. Wilson saw Brown put his hand down to his right hip, and initially assumed the bullet went through the door and struck Brown there. Wilson then described Brown becoming enraged, and that Brown "looked like a demon." Brown then leaned into the driver's window so that his head and arms were inside the SUV and he assaulted Wilson again. Wilson explained that while blocking his face with his left hand, he tried to fire his gun with his right hand, but the gun jammed. Wilson lifted the gun, without looking, and used both hands to manually clear the gun while also trying to shield himself. He then successfully fired another shot, holding the gun in his right hand. According to Wilson, he could not see where he shot, but did not think that he struck Brown because he saw "smoke" outside the window, seemingly from the ground, indicating to him a point of impact that was farther away.

Brown then took off running. Wilson radioed for additional assistance, calling out that shots were fired. Wilson then chased after Brown on foot. Federal prosecutors questioned Wilson as to why he did not drive away or wait for backup, but instead chose to pursue Brown despite the attack he just described. Wilson explained that he ran after Brown because Brown posed a danger to others, having just assaulted a police officer and likely stolen from Ferguson Market. Given Brown's violent and otherwise erratic behavior, Wilson was concerned that Brown was a danger to anyone who crossed his path as he ran.

Wilson denied firing any shots while Brown was running from him. Rather he kept his gun out, but down in a "low ready" position. Wilson explained that he chased after Brown, repeatedly yelling at him to stop and get on the ground. Brown kept running, but when he was about 20 to 30 feet from Wilson, abruptly stopped, and turned around toward Wilson, appearing "psychotic," "hostile," and "crazy," as though he was "looking through" Wilson. While making

---

[5] According to Wilson's sergeant, Witness 147, Wilson told him that Brown made that comment later when Brown was charging at Wilson in the roadway. Witness 147 remembered this part of Wilson's account when he testified before the county grand jury, and not when he was interviewed by state and federal authorities. In every other account, Wilson stated that Brown made that comment as soon as he withdrew his gun.
[6] During his second interview with SLCPD detectives, Wilson stated he was unsure with which hand Brown reached for Wilson's gun. During all other statements, when asked, Wilson said that Brown used his right hand.

a "grunting noise" and with what Wilson described as the "most intense aggressive face" that he had ever seen on a person, Brown then made a hop-like movement, similar to what a person does when he starts running. Brown then started running at Wilson, closing the distance between them to about 15 feet. Wilson explained that he again feared for his life, and backed up as Brown came toward him, repeatedly ordering Brown to stop and get on the ground. Brown failed to comply and kept coming at Wilson. Wilson explained that he knew if Brown reached him, he "would be done." During Brown's initial strides, Brown put his right hand in what appeared to be his waistband, albeit covered by his shirt. Wilson thought Brown might be reaching for a weapon. Wilson fired multiple shots. Brown paused. Wilson explained that he then paused, again yelled for Brown to get on the ground, and again Brown charged at him, hand in waistband. Wilson backed up and fired again. The same thing happened a third time where Brown very briefly paused, and Wilson paused and yelled for Brown to get on the ground. Brown continued to "charge." Wilson described having tunnel vision on Brown's right arm, all the while backing up as Brown approached, not understanding why Brown had yet to stop. Wilson fired the last volley of shots when Brown was about eight to ten feet from him. When Wilson fired the last shot, he saw the bullet go into Brown's head, and Brown "went down right there." Wilson initially estimated that on the roadway, he fired five shots and then two shots, none of which had any effect on Brown. Then Brown leaned forward as though he was getting ready to "tackle" Wilson, and Wilson fired the last shot.

Federal prosecutors questioned Wilson about his actions after the shooting. Wilson explained that he never touched Brown's body. Using the microphone on his shoulder, Wilson radioed, "Send me every car we got and a supervisor." Within seconds, additional officers and his sergeant arrived on scene. In response to specific questions by federal prosecutors, Wilson explained that he had left his keys in the ignition of his vehicle and the engine running during the pursuit, so he went back to his SUV to secure it. In so doing, he was careful only to touch the door and the keys. Wilson then walked over to his sergeant, Witness 147, and told him what happened.[7] Both Wilson and Witness 147 explained that Witness 147 told Wilson to wait in his SUV, but Wilson refused, explaining that if he waited there, it would be known to the neighborhood that he was the shooter. Wilson explained that the atmosphere was quickly becoming hostile, and he either needed to be put to work with his fellow officers or he needed to leave. Per Witness 147's orders, Wilson drove Witness 147's vehicle to the FPD. It was during the drive that Wilson realized he was not bleeding, but had what he thought was Brown's blood on both hands.

As soon as Wilson got to the police department, he scrubbed both hands. When federal prosecutors challenged why he did so in light of the potential evidentiary value, Wilson explained that he realized after the fact that he should not have done so, but at the time he was reacting to a potential biohazard while still under the stress of the moment. Wilson then rendered his gun safe and packaged it with the one remaining round in an evidence envelope. When federal prosecutors further questioned why he packaged his own gun, Wilson explained that he wanted to ensure its preservation for analysis because it would prove what happened. At first, he hoped Brown's fingerprints or epithelial DNA from sweat on his hand might be present from when Brown grabbed the gun. But then Wilson actually saw blood on the gun, and

---

[7] According to Witness 147, he spoke to Wilson while Wilson was seated in his SUV.

assumed that since he was not bleeding, the blood likely belonged to Brown, and therefore, Brown's DNA would be present.

During Wilson's interview with federal authorities, prosecutors and agents focused on whether he was consistent with his previous statements, the motivation for his actions, and his training and experience relative to when the use of deadly force is appropriate. Federal prosecutors challenged Wilson with specificity about why he stopped Brown and whether he was aware that Brown and Witness 101 were suspects in the Ferguson Market robbery. Similarly, prosecutors challenged Wilson about his decision to use deadly force inside the SUV, to chase after Brown, and to again use deadly force on Brown in the roadway. Wilson responded to those challenges in a credible manner, offering reasonable explanations to the questions posed.

At the time of his interview, federal prosecutors and agents were aware of the autopsy, DNA, and ballistics results, as detailed below. Wilson's account was consistent with those results, and consistent with the accounts of other independent eyewitnesses, whose accounts were also consistent with the physical evidence. Wilson's statements were consistent with each other in all material ways, and would not be subject to effective impeachment for inconsistencies or deviation from the physical evidence.[8] Therefore, in analyzing all of the evidence, federal prosecutors found Wilson's account to be credible.

B. Physical and Forensic Evidence

1. Crime Scene

As noted above, SLCPD detectives from the Bureau of Criminal Identification, Crime Scene Unit processed the scene of the shootings. During processing, they photographed and took video of the crime scene, including Brown's body and Wilson's SUV. They measured distances from Brown's body, Wilson's SUV, and various pieces of evidence. As described in detail below, they recovered twelve spent shell casings.[9] One was located on the ground between the driver's door and back passenger door of the SUV and another was located near the sidewalk, diagonally across from the driver's door. Seven casings and one spent projectile were located in the general vicinity of Brown's body. Those casings were located on the ground next to the left side of his body (on the south side of Canfield Drive), with four closer to his body, and three in the grassy area of the sidewalk. The projectile was located on the right side of Brown's body (on the north side of Canfield Drive). Three additional casings were further east, or further away from where Brown came to rest. Crime scene detectives also recovered a spent projectile fragment from the wall of an apartment building located east of Brown's body, in the direction

---

[8] Federal prosecutors were aware of and reviewed prior complaints against Wilson, as well as media reports, alleging Wilson engaged in misconduct. Such allegations were not substantiated, and do not contain information admissible in federal court in support of a prosecution.

[9] The locations of the shell casings are consistent with Wilson's account and the credible witness accounts. However, shell casings provide limited evidentiary value relative to the precise location of the shooter and bullet trajectory because they tend to bounce and roll unpredictably after being ejected from the firearm and before coming to rest.

toward which Wilson had been shooting.[10] As described below, crime scene detectives noted apparent blood[11] in the roadway approximately 17 feet and 22 feet east of where Brown's body was found and east of the casings that were recovered, consistent with Brown moving toward Wilson before his death. There was no other blood found in the roadway, other than the pool of blood surrounding Brown's body.

Crime scene detectives recovered Brown's St. Louis Cardinals baseball cap by the driver's door of the SUV. Two bracelets, one black and yellow, and the other beaded, were found on either side of the SUV.[12] Brown's Nike flip flops were located in the roadway, the left one near the front of the driver's side of the vehicle, approximately 126 feet west of where Brown's head came to rest, and the right one in the center of the roadway, 82.5 feet west of where Brown's head came to rest and just south of the center line. This is consistent with witness descriptions that Brown, wearing his socks, described as bright yellow with a marijuana leaf pattern, ran diagonally away from the SUV, crossing over the center line.

Prior to transport of Brown's body, the SLCME medicolegal investigator documented the position of Brown's body on the ground. Brown was on his stomach with his right cheek on the ground, his buttocks partially in the air. His uninjured left arm was back and partially bent under his body with his left hand at his waistband, balled up in a fist. His injured right arm was back behind him, almost at his right side, with his injured right hand at hip level, palm up. Brown's shorts were midway down his buttocks, as though they had partially fallen down.

The forensic analysis of the seized evidence is detailed below:

2. Autopsy Findings

There were three autopsies conducted on Michael Brown's body. SLCME conducted the first autopsy. A private forensic pathologist conducted the second autopsy at the request of Brown's family. AFMES conducted the third autopsy at the Department's request.

The SLCME, AFMES, and the private forensic pathologist were consistent in their findings unless otherwise noted. Brown was shot at least six and at most eight times. As described below, two entrance wounds may have been re-entry wounds, accounting for why the number of shots that struck Brown is not definite.

Of the eight gunshot wounds, two wounds, a penetrating gunshot wound to the apex of Brown's head, and a graze or tangential wound to the base of Brown's right thumb, have the most significant evidentiary value when determining the prosecutive merit of this matter. The former is significant because the gunshot to the head would have almost immediately

---

[10] Crime scene detectives also noted a hole in the wall of an apartment building located on the south side of Canfield Drive, east of Wilson's SUV. They removed a small section of siding, but were unable to determine whether there was a projectile within the wall without causing significant structural damage to the building. There is no evidence to indicate what caused the hole or when it was made.

[11] As noted below, the blood in the roadway was determined to be Brown's blood.

[12] It was never determined to whom these bracelets belong or when they were left in the street.

incapacitated and immobilized Brown; the latter is significant because it is consistent with Brown's hand being in close range or having near-contact with the muzzle of Wilson's gun and corroborates Wilson's account that Brown struggled with him to gain control of the gun in the SUV.

The skin tags, or flaps of skin created by the graze of the bullet associated with the right thumb wound, indicate bullet trajectory. They were oriented toward the tip of the right thumb, indicating the path of the bullet went from the tip of the thumb toward the base. Microscopic analysis of the wound indicates that Brown's hand was near the muzzle of the gun when Wilson pulled the trigger. Both AFMES and SLCME pathologists observed numerous deposits of dark particulate foreign debris, consistent with gunpowder soot from the muzzle of the gun embedded in and around the wound. The private forensic pathologist called it gunshot residue, opining that Brown's right hand was less than a foot from the gun. The SLCME pathologist opined that the muzzle of the gun was likely six to nine inches from Brown's hand when it fired. AFMES pathologists opined that the particulate matter was, in fact, soot and was found at the exact point of entry of the wound. The soot, along with the thermal change in the skin resulting from heat discharge of the firearm, indicates that the base of Brown's right hand was within inches of the muzzle of Wilson's gun when it fired. AFMES pathologists further opined that, given the tangential nature of the wound, the fact that the soot was concentrated on one side of the wound, and the bullet trajectory as detailed below, the wound to the thumb is consistent with Brown's hand being on the barrel of the gun itself, though not the muzzle, at the time the shot was fired.

The presence of soot also proves that the wound to the thumb was the result of the gunshot at the SUV.[13] As detailed below, several witnesses described Brown at or in Wilson's SUV when the first shot was fired, and a bullet was recovered from within the driver's door of the SUV. There is no evidence that Wilson was within inches of Brown's thumb other than in the SUV at the outset of the incident. Additionally, according to the SLCME pathologist and the private forensic pathologist, a piece of Brown's skin recovered from the exterior of the driver's door of the SUV is consistent with skin from the part of Brown's thumb that was wounded. It is therefore a virtual certainty that the first shot fired was the one that caused the tangential thumb wound.

The order of the remaining shots cannot be determined, though the shot to Brown's head would have killed him where he stood, preventing him from making any additional purposeful movement toward Wilson after the final shots were fired.[14] The fatal bullet entered the skull, the brain, and the base of the skull, and came to rest in the soft tissues of the right face. The trajectory of the bullet was downward, forward, and to the right. Brown could not have been standing straight when Wilson fired this bullet because Wilson is slightly shorter than Brown. Brown was likely bent at the waist or falling forward when he received this wound. It is also possible, although not consistent with credible eyewitness accounts, that Brown had fallen to his knees with his head forward when Wilson fired this shot. However, the lack of stippling and soot indicates that Wilson was at least two to three feet from Brown when he fired.

---

[13] Soot typically appears if the muzzle is within less than one foot of the target and stippling typically appears if the muzzle is within two to three feet of the target.
[14] This fact was critical for prosecutors in evaluating the credibility of witness accounts that stated that Brown continued moving toward Wilson after Wilson ceased firing shots.

The remaining gunshots, like the thumb wound, were all on Brown's right side and none of them would have necessarily immediately immobilized Brown. The lack of soot and stippling indicates that the shots were fired from a distance of at least two to three feet. However, as described below, because of environmental conditions and because Brown's shirt was blood soaked, it was not suitable for gunshot residue analysis to determine muzzle-to-target distance. Therefore, we cannot reliably say whether gunshot residue on Brown's shirt might have provided evidence of muzzle-to-target distance. Regardless, gunshot residue is inherently delicate and easily transferrable. [15]

In addition to the thumb wound and the fatal shot to the head, Brown sustained a gunshot wound to his central forehead, with a corresponding exit wound of the right jaw. The bullet tracked through the right eye and right orbital bone, causing fractures of the facial bones. Brown sustained another gunshot wound to the upper right chest, near the neck. The bullet tracked though the right clavicle and upper lobe of the right lung, and came to rest in the right chest. Brown sustained another entrance wound to his lateral right chest. The bullet tracked through and fractured the eighth right rib, puncturing the lower lobe of the right lung. The bullet was recovered from the soft tissue of the right back. The AFMES pathologists and the private forensic pathologist opined that the right chest wound could have been a re-entry wound from an arm wound as described below, and the clavicle wound could have been a re-entry wound from the bullet that entered Brown's forehead and exited his jaw. The SLCME pathologist also allowed for the possibility of re-entry wounds, but did not opine with specificity due to the variability of such wounds.

Brown also sustained a gunshot wound to the front of the upper right arm, near the armpit, with a corresponding gunshot exit wound of the back of the upper right arm. The remaining gunshot wounds were also to the right arm. These bullet trajectories are described according to the standard anatomic diagram, that is, standing, arms at sides, palms facing forward. That said, Brown sustained a gunshot wound to the dorsal (back) right forearm, below the elbow. The bullet tracked through the bone in the forearm, fracturing it, and exiting through the ventral (front) right forearm. Finally, Brown sustained a tangential or graze gunshot wound to the right bicep, above the elbow.

Given the mobility of the arm, it is impossible to determine the position of the body relative to the shooter at the time the arm wounds were inflicted. Therefore, the autopsy results do not indicate whether Brown was facing Wilson or had his back to him. They do not indicate whether Brown sustained those two arm wounds while his hands were up, down, or by his waistband. The private forensic pathologist opined that he would expect a re-entry wound across Brown's stomach if Brown's hand was at his waistband at the time Wilson fired. However, as mentioned, there is no way to know the exact position of Brown's arm relative to his waistband

---

[15] Although Brown's shirt was blood soaked, the private forensic pathologist noted the following with regard to Brown's shorts and socks, "Examination of the clothing…shows small dried blood drops on his khaki shorts and yellow socks most consistent with drops from the hand wound." This was significant to prosecutors because it is not inconsistent with Brown lowering his hands and/or putting his hand(s) near his waistband.

at the time the bullets struck. Therefore, these gunshot wounds neither corroborate nor discredit Wilson's account or the account of any other witness. However, the concentration of bullet wounds on Brown's right side is consistent with Wilson's description that he focused on Brown's right arm while shooting.

The autopsy established that Brown did not sustain gunshot wounds to his back.[16] There was no evidence to corroborate that Wilson choked, strangled, or tightly grasped Brown on or around his neck, as described by Witness 101 in the summary of his account below. There were no bruises, abrasions, hemorrhaging of soft tissues, or any other injuries to the neck, nor was there evidence of petechial hemorrhaging of Brown's remaining left eye. The private forensic pathologist opined that although the lack of injury does not signify the absence of strangulation, it would be "surprising," given Brown's size, if Wilson attempted to strangle Brown. The private forensic pathologist explained that the act of strangling is often committed by the stronger person, as it is rarely effective if attempted by the person of smaller size or weaker strength.[17]

Brown sustained a one inch superficial incised wound to the right middle of the front of his left arm. SCLME differed with AFMES, characterizing this wound as an abrasion, but AFMES opined that this was more like a cut, consistent with being caused by broken window glass. Brown also sustained abrasions to the right side of the head and face, including abrasions near the right forehead, the lateral right face, and the upper right cheek, consistent with Brown falling and impacting the ground with his face. The private forensic pathologist opined that the severity of these abrasions could have been caused by involuntary seizures as Brown died. He also opined, as did the SLCME pathologist, that these abrasions were consistent with Brown impacting the ground upon death and sliding on the roadway due to the momentum from quickly moving forward.

According to the AFMES and SCLME pathologists, Brown also had small knuckle abrasions, but the pathologists could not link them to any specific source. The SLCME pathologist opined they may have been inflicted post mortem, while the AFMES pathologist opined that they were too small to determine whether they were caused pre or post-mortem.[18] The private forensic pathologist did not note any knuckle abrasions or injury to Brown's hands, explaining that he would expect Brown to have knuckle injury if Wilson sustained broken bones, but not necessarily bruising. AFMES pathologists likewise concurred that lack of injury to Brown's hands is not inconsistent with bruising to Wilson's face.

    3. <u>DNA Analysis</u>

---

[16] This evidence was significant to prosecutors when determining the credibility of those witness accounts that stated that Wilson shot Brown in the back.

[17] This evidence was significant to prosecutors when determining the credibility of those witness accounts that stated that Wilson choked or grabbed Brown by the neck at the outset of the struggle at the SUV.

[18] Post mortem abrasions are consistent with Brown's hands hitting the ground after the final shot to the vortex of the head. It is less likely that they were inflicted during removal of Brown's body because Brown's hands were secured in brown paper bags prior to transport.

The SLCPD Crime Laboratory conducted DNA analysis on swabs taken from Wilson, Brown, Wilson's gun, and the crime scene. Brown's DNA was found at four significant locations: on Wilson's gun; on the roadway further away from where he died; on the SUV driver's door and inside the driver's cabin area of the SUV; and on Wilson's clothes. A DNA mixture from which Wilson's DNA could not be excluded was found on Brown's left palm.

Analysis of DNA on Wilson's gun revealed a major mixture profile that is 2.1 octillion times more likely a mixture of DNA from Wilson and DNA from Brown than from Wilson and anyone else. This is conclusive evidence that Brown's DNA was on Wilson's gun.[19]

Brown is the source of the DNA found in two bloodstains on Canfield Drive, approximately 17 and 22 feet east of where Brown fell to his death, proving that Brown moved forward toward Wilson prior to the fatal shot to his head.

Brown's DNA was found both on the inside and outside of the driver's side of the SUV. Brown is the source of DNA in blood found on the exterior of the passenger door of the driver's side of the SUV. Likewise, a piece of Brown's skin was recovered from the exterior of the driver's door of the SUV, consistent with Brown sustaining injury while at that door. Brown is also the source of the major contributor of a DNA mixture found on the interior driver's door handle of the SUV. A DNA mixture obtained from the top of the exterior of the driver's door revealed a major mixture profile that is 6.9 million times more likely a mixture of DNA from Wilson and DNA from Brown than from Wilson and anyone else.

Brown's DNA was found on Wilson's uniform shirt collar and pants. With respect to the left side of Wilson's shirt and collar, it is 2.1 trillion times more likely that the recovered DNA mixture is DNA from Wilson and DNA from Brown than from Wilson and anyone else. Similarly, with respect to a DNA mixture obtained from the left side of Wilson's pants, it is 34 sextillion times more likely that the mixture is DNA from Wilson and DNA from Brown than from Wilson and anyone else. Brown is also the source of the major male profile found in a DNA mixture found in a bloodstain on the upper left thigh of Wilson's pants.

DNA analysis of Brown's left palm revealed a DNA mixture with Brown as the major contributor, and Wilson being 98 times more likely the minor contributor than anyone else.

DNA analysis of Brown's clothes, right hand, fingernails, and clothes excluded Wilson as a possible contributor.

4. Dispatch Recordings

---

[19] While it is possible that Wilson inadvertently transferred Brown's blood from his own hand to his gun either after the struggle or while packaging his gun (even though Wilson claimed to have already washed his hands), such a possibility is speculative. The autopsy results and bullet trajectory are consistent with Brown's DNA being present on the gun as a result of the struggle over the gun. Regardless, the absence of Brown's DNA on Wilson's gun would not change the prosecutive decision.

According to FPD records, at about 11:53 a.m., a dispatcher called out a "stealing in progress" at the address of Ferguson Market while Wilson was in the midst of a sick infant call. During his interview with federal officials, Wilson told prosecutors and agents that he heard the call on his portable radio, but did not hear the specifics about the location of the "stealing in progress." He also stated that he heard that one of the suspects was wearing a "black shirt," that they had stolen cigarillos, and were going toward the Quick-Trip. The actual description given was that of a "black male in a white t-shirt," "running toward the Quick-Trip," and that "he took a whole box of Swisher cigars." Two officers, Witness 145 and Witness 146, the same two FPD officers who first responded to Canfield Drive after the shooting, responded to the Ferguson Market. At approximately 11:56 a.m., Witness 145, via radio, added, "He's with another male. He's got a red Cardinals hat, white t-shirt, yellow socks, and khaki shorts."

Wilson left the sick call at approximately 11:58 a.m., after EMS arrived to transport the mother and sick child to the hospital. Twenty-seven seconds later, Wilson radioed to Witness 145 and Witness 146, "Do you guys need me?," corroborating that Wilson was aware of the theft at Ferguson Market prior to his encounter with Brown. Witness 145 responded that the suspect "disappeared into the woodwork." Wilson, having not heard him, asked the dispatcher to "relay." The dispatcher then clarified, "He thinks that they…disappeared." Wilson then said "clear," indicating that he understood.

Wilson drove his police SUV west on Canfield Drive, where he encountered Brown and Witness 101 walking east in the middle of the street. Wilson's last recorded radio transmission occurred at approximately noon when he called out, "Put me on Canfield with two and send me another car," consistent with Wilson's account that he radioed for backup once he interacted with Brown and Witness 101.

Several radio transmissions followed from dispatch and from Officer 145 seeking a response from Wilson to no avail. About one minute and forty seconds following Wilson's last transmission, Witness 145 called out to send the supervising sergeant to Canfield Drive and Copper Creek Court, the location of the shooting incident. There were no recorded radio transmissions from Wilson from the time Wilson called for assistance to the time that Witness 145 called for a supervisor.

As noted above, Wilson stated that he also radioed for backup after the initial shots when Brown ran from the SUV, and then again after he shot Brown to death. According to Wilson, as he left the shooting scene, he realized that his radio must have switched from channel 1, which he had been using, to channel 3 during the initial struggle. Channel 3 is a dedicated channel for the North County Fire Department. It only receives transmissions, and therefore, officers cannot use that channel to transmit messages to dispatch. While this is not definitive evidence that Wilson attempted to call for assistance both after the initial shots in the SUV and after he killed Brown, it offers a plausible explanation for the lack of radio transmissions. Moreover, as detailed below, there are several witnesses who state that Wilson paused in the SUV after Brown took off running, arguably giving him enough time to attempt to radio dispatch. Likewise, several witnesses saw Wilson appear to use his shoulder microphone after Brown fell to the ground, presumably to radio dispatch.

5. Ballistics

Witness 143, a firearms and toolmarks examiner with the SLCPD, conducted the ballistics analysis for the St. Louis County Police Laboratory. Witness 144, an FBI firearms and toolmarks examiner, conducted gunshot residue analysis and reconstructed the shooting incident.

i. *Wilson's Firearm and Projectiles Fired*

There were a total of five projectiles, and a fragment from another projectile, recovered from the crime scene and Brown's autopsy. There were a total of 12 shell casings recovered from the crime scene. Wilson's gun can hold up to 13 rounds, 12 in the magazine and one in the chamber. Witness 143 test-fired Wilson's Sig Sauer S&W .40 caliber semi-automatic pistol, noting apparent blood on the gun. He compared the test bullets and casings to those seized as evidence from Brown's body and the crime scene. Witness 143 confirmed that all 12 shell casings were fired from Wilson's gun, consistent with the one round remaining in the gun after the shooting. Witness 143 also confirmed that four of the recovered projectiles, as well as the recovered fragment, were fired from Wilson's gun. The remaining projectile, recovered from the inside of the driver's door of Wilson's SUV, was too damaged to conclusively find that it came from Wilson's gun.

ii. *Projectile Recovered from SUV*

Witness 144 conducted a shooting incident reconstruction of the interior driver's door panel of Wilson's SUV to determine the trajectory of the bullet that was recovered there. The trajectory of the bullet was at a downward angle from left to right, striking the armrest near the interior door handle, entering the door from inside the SUV, and coming to rest inside the door. This is consistent with Wilson's description of the initial gunshot.

Witness 144 conducted gunshot residue analysis on the inside of the driver's door. Particulate and vaporous lead residues found on the interior driver's door panel near the interior window weather stripping and on the interior side frame of the driver's door were, like the recovery of the bullet itself, consistent with the discharge of a firearm. These residues were unsuitable for muzzle-to-target distance determinations. However, vaporous lead residues rarely are deposited at a distance greater than 24 inches, consistent with Wilson discharging his firearm while seated in the driver's seat, less than two feet from the driver's door.

iii. *Gunshot Residue on Brown's Shirt*

Witness 144 conducted gunshot residue analysis on Brown's shirt. For the most part, gunshot residue analysis can only determine whether defects in an item, *i.e.,* the holes in his shirt, are the result of gunshots. Analysis cannot determine the directional travel of bullets.

Witness 144 examined seven holes in the shirt. Gunshot residues in the form of nitrite and bullet wipe lead residues were found near some of the holes. This does not necessarily suggest that the remaining holes were not created by bullets. According to Witness 144, lack of gunshot residue could be due to the possibility of intervening conditions, like large amounts of blood, environmental conditions, or the way the shirt was folded and packaged.

Likewise, the presence of nitrite residues tells very little. Nitrite residues were found near three holes in Brown's right sleeve, and one hole in the right chest of this shirt. Test-firing of the gun showed that nitrite residues appear at a muzzle-to-target distance of eight feet or less, consistent with Wilson's description and several other witness descriptions that Wilson and Brown were about eight feet apart during the final shots. However, the residues were not in a measurable pattern. This means that they may not even be associated with the specific holes in the shirt that they are near, but rather may be just indiscriminate residue from any of the shots, including the close range shots at the SUV, or transferred from one shot to another during the handling and packaging of the clothes.

6. Fingerprints

Wilson's gun was not tested for the presence of Brown's fingerprints. After SLCPD crime scene detectives recovered Wilson's gun, they submitted the gun for DNA analysis rather than for fingerprints analysis. The detectives told federal prosecutors that they knew that typically testing for one would preclude testing for the other, and there was a high likelihood of DNA given the presence of apparent blood on the gun. They also knew that even according to Wilson, Brown never had sole possession of the gun, and if Brown ever had control of the gun at all, it was only when Brown's hand was over Wilson's hand during a struggle for the gun, lessening the likelihood of fingerprints. Furthermore, based on their training and experience, there was a greater likelihood of finding a DNA profile on the gun than lifting fingerprints with enough fine ridge detail to make it suitable for comparison.[20] Because the gun was swabbed in its entirety, it could not later undergo latent fingerprint analysis.[21]

SLCPD crime scene detectives lifted five latent fingerprints from the outside of the driver's door of the SUV. Two were unsuitable for comparison; one was determined to be Wilson's fingerprint; and the remaining two prints, although suitable for comparison, belonged to neither Brown nor Wilson. The leather interior of the SUV was unsuitable for recovering latent prints. Fingerprint examiners also tested Wilson's duty belt for fingerprints, but none recovered was suitable for comparison.

7. Audio Recording of Shots Fired

Witness 136 was in his apartment using a video chat application on his mobile phone when the shooting occurred. According to Witness 136, he heard "maybe three" gunshots followed by a five to six second pause. After those first gunshots, Witness 136 recorded the remainder of his chat and turned it over to the FBI. The recording is about 12 seconds long and captured a total of 10 gunshots. The gunshots begin after the first four seconds. The recording

---

[20] The grips and hammer, the latter of which was where blood was recovered on Wilson's gun, are textured, making it difficult to lift latent prints.

[21] Fingerprint analysis would not have changed the prosecutive decision. Had the gun yielded Brown's fingerprints, such evidence would further corroborate Wilson's account. If the gun did not test positive for Brown's fingerprints, the state of the evidence would remain the same.

then captured six gunshots in two seconds. There was a three second pause, followed by a seventh gunshot. There was a quick pause of less than one second before the final three-shot volley within two seconds. The recording was not time-stamped. As detailed below, this recording is consistent with several credible witness accounts as well as Wilson's account, that he fired several volleys of shots, briefly pausing between each one.

8. Wilson's Medical Records

Paramedics examined Wilson when he returned to the FPD after the shooting, and recommended that he go to the hospital for follow-up treatment. Wilson sought medical treatment at Christian Northwest Hospital within two hours of the shooting. Witness 117, a nurse practitioner, examined Wilson. For the purpose of making a medical diagnosis, Witness 117 questioned Wilson about what happened. Wilson stated that he was twice punched in the jaw. Witness 117 noted acute or fresh pink scratch marks on the back of Wilson's neck as well as swelling to his jaw. Wilson sustained a contusion of the mandibular joint or jaw area, but did not break his jaw or any other bones. According to Witness 117, Wilson's injuries were consistent with his description of what transpired.

Wilson submitted to a drug and alcohol screen. His blood alcohol content was 0.00% and he tested negative for cocaine, marijuana metabolites, amphetamines, opiates, and phencyclidine, the chemical commonly known as PCP.

9. Brown's Toxicology

A toxicologist with the St. Louis University (SLU) Toxicology Laboratory and the Chief of the Division of Forensic Toxicology at AFMES each conducted blood and urine screens on samples collected from Brown's body. Brown tested positive for the presence of cannabinoids, the hallucinogenic substances associated with marijuana use. The SLU Toxicology Laboratory found 12 nanograms per milliliter of Delta-9-THC, the active ingredient in marijuana, where AFMES found 11 nanograms per milliliter of Delta-9-THC in Brown's blood.

According to both laboratories, these levels of Delta-9-THC are consistent with Brown having ingested THC within a few hours before his death. This concentration of THC would have rendered Brown impaired at the time of his death. As a general matter, this level of impairment can alter one's perception of time and space, but the extent to which this was true in Brown's case cannot be determined. THC affects individuals differently depending on unknown variables such as whether Brown was a chronic user and the concentration of the THC ingested.

10. Ferguson Market Surveillance Video

At approximately 11:53 a.m. on August 9, 2014, about ten minutes prior to the shooting, Brown and Witness 101 went to Ferguson Market, a nearby convenience store. Surveillance video shows Brown stealing several packages of cigarillos and then forcefully shoving the store clerk who tried to stop him from leaving the store without paying. Evidence of this theft and assault likely would be admissible by the defense in a prosecution of Wilson because it is relevant to show Brown's state of mind at or near the time of the shooting, and arguably corroborates Wilson's self-defense claim.

Surveillance cameras captured the incident without audio. SLCPD detectives, FBI agents, and federal prosecutors jointly interviewed the store employees who were present at the time. The employees, a father (the clerk who was assaulted) and his adult daughter, are of Indian origin. The father does not speak English well, and therefore, was not as able as his daughter to recount with specificity what Brown said during the incident.

The video depicts Brown and Witness 101 entering the store and proceeding to the front counter. Brown stood at the register, as Witness 101 waited behind him. Brown asked the clerk behind the counter for cigarillos. The clerk put a package of cigarillos on the counter. Brown then "snatched" the package of cigarillos from the counter. Using his left hand, Brown reached behind him and gave them to Witness 101.[22] Brown then reached over the counter, as Witness 101 described and the video shows, and took additional packages of cigarillos. In so doing, Brown dropped some of the cigarillos and had an exchange with the clerk during which he refused to pay. Witness 101 then placed the cigarillos that Brown had given him back on the register counter, as Brown picked up his stolen goods from the floor.

Brown and Witness 101 proceeded to the exit and the clerk, who is about 5'6" and 150 lbs, attempted to stop them. The clerk first tried to hold the store door closed to prevent Brown's exit. However, Brown shoved the clerk aside, and as Witness 101 walked out the door, Brown menacingly re-approached the clerk. According to the store employees, Brown, looking "crazy" and using profane language, said something like, "What are you gonna do about it?" Brown then exited the store and the clerk's daughter called 911.

C. **Witness Accounts**

As the first responding investigators, SLCPD detectives interviewed witnesses on Canfield Drive within the first few hours of the shooting. One week later, on August 16, 2014, in an effort to identify additional witnesses who may have been reluctant to speak with local law enforcement, the FBI conducted a neighborhood canvass of more than 300 residences. Federal and county authorities largely conducted additional interviews jointly, unless a witness expressed discomfort with the presence of either federal agents or SLCPD detectives. To evaluate the merits of a potential federal prosecution, federal prosecutors and FBI agents conducted follow-up interviews. Many witnesses also testified before the county grand jury. Unless otherwise noted, witnesses did not know, or know of, Brown or Wilson prior to the shooting.

For ease of review, this report divides the summaries of witness accounts into three sections based on the nature and credibility of their accounts to a jury. First, the report summarizes the accounts of those witnesses whose statements have been materially consistent, are consistent with the physical evidence, and that are mutually corroborative. For these reasons, prosecutors determined these witness accounts were reliable and would be credible to jurors. This section is further broken down into subsections for those witness accounts that support Wilson's claim of self-defense and those that support a criminal prosecution of Wilson. Of

---

[22] Brown's actions on the surveillance video at that moment mimicked the way in which Wilson described Brown again handing the cigarillos to Witness 101 minutes later as Brown assaulted Wilson in the SUV.

course, to support a prosecution of Wilson under 18 U.S.C. § 242, the weight of the evidence from those witness accounts that support a prosecution must be prove the violation beyond a reasonable doubt to twelve reasonable jurors. A prosecution will fail if the credible evidence creates "reasonable doubt" of Wilson's guilt by supporting Wilson's statements that he acted reasonably and in self-defense. The second section of summaries contains those accounts that neither inculpate Wilson nor fully corroborate Wilson's account. These witnesses, regardless of whether prosecutors determined their accounts to be credible, would not strengthen the government's case in a prosecution of Wilson. The third section of summaries contains those witness accounts that are inconsistent with the physical and forensic evidence, materially inconsistent with that witness's own prior statements, or those witnesses who have recanted large portions of their accounts, admitting that they did not in fact witness the shooting as they initially claimed. Therefore, for this last category of witnesses, federal prosecutors either could not rely on their accounts to support a prosecution of Darren Wilson or did not consider their accounts in making a prosecutive decision.

1. Witnesses Materially Consistent with Prior Statements, Physical Evidence, and Other Witnesses and Therefore, Give Credible Accounts

i. *Witnesses Materially Consistent with Prior Statements, Physical Evidence, and Other Witnesses Who Corroborate That Wilson Acted in Self-Defense*

a. **Witness 102**

Witness 102 is a 27-year-old bi-racial male. Witness 102 gave three statements. First, SLCPD detectives interviewed him; second, FBI agents interviewed him; third, Witness 102 testified before the county grand jury.

Witness 102 was doing house repairs on a residence on Canfield Drive when the shooting occurred. Witness 102 first noticed Brown and Witness 101 walking down Canfield Drive about 20 minutes prior to the shooting when he went to his truck to retrieve a broom. Brown's size initially drew Witness 102's attention. When Witness 102 later came back outside to get another tool, he noticed Wilson's SUV parked in the middle of the street at an angle, with the driver's side closer to the center of the street. Witness 102's vantage point was street level, about 450 feet from the SUV with a view of the driver's side of the SUV.

According to Witness 102, he saw Brown standing on the driver's side of the SUV, bent over with his body through the driver's window from the waist up. Witness 102 explained that Brown was "wrestling" through the window, but he was unable to see what Wilson was doing. After a few seconds, Witness 102 heard a gunshot. Immediately, Brown took off running in the opposite direction from where Witness 102 was standing. Witness 102 heard something metallic hit the ground. Witness 102 thought that he had just witnessed the murder of a police officer because a few seconds passed before Wilson emerged from the SUV. Wilson then chased Brown with his gun drawn, but not pointed at Brown, until Brown abruptly turned around at a nearby driveway. Witness 102 explained that it made no sense to him why Brown turned around. Brown did not get on the ground or put his hands up in surrender. In fact, Witness 102 told investigators that he knew "for sure that [Brown's] hands were not above his head." Rather,

Brown made some type of movement similar to pulling his pants up or a shoulder shrug, and then "charged" at Wilson. It was only then that Wilson fired five or six shots at Brown. Brown paused and appeared to flinch, and Wilson stopped firing. However, Brown charged at Wilson again, and again Wilson fired about three or four rounds until Brown finally collapsed on the ground. Witness 102 was in disbelief that Wilson seemingly kept missing because Brown kept advancing forward. Witness 102 described Brown as a "threat," moving at a "full charge." Witness 102 stated that Wilson only fired shots when Brown was coming toward Wilson. It appeared to Witness 102 that Wilson's life was in jeopardy. Witness 102 was unable to hear whether Brown or Wilson said anything.

Witness 102 did not see Brown's friend, Witness 101, at any time during the incident until Witness 101 "came out of nowhere," shouting, "'They just killed him!'" Witness 101 seemed to be shouting toward a blue Monte Carlo[23] that had stopped behind Wilson's SUV. Witness 101 then ran off. Witness 102 explained that once he saw officers putting up police tape, he went down to the scene and began telling another onlooker what he had witnessed. Witness 102 later learned via a "friend" on Facebook that his voice was inadvertently captured on another bystander's cell phone recording. Federal prosecutors reviewed this recording and Witness 102 identified his voice on the recording when he testified before the county grand jury. In it, Witness 102 can be heard correcting someone else who was recounting what he heard from others, that Wilson "stood over [Brown] and shot while on the ground." In response, Witness 102 stated that Wilson shot Brown because Brown came back toward Wilson. Witness 102 "kept thinking" that Wilson's shots were "missing" Brown because Brown kept moving.

Witness 102 did not stay on Canfield Drive long after the shooting, but rather started to leave the area after about five minutes because he felt uncomfortable. According to Witness 102, crowds of people had begun to gather, wrongly claiming the police shot Brown for no reason and that he had his hands up in surrender. Two black women approached Witness 102, mobile phones set to record, asking him to recount what he had witnessed. Witness 102 responded that they would not like what he had to say. The women responded with racial slurs, calling him names like "white motherfucker."

Witness 102 called 911 the following day to report what he saw. He then went to the FPD on Monday, August 11, 2014, where he was referred to the SLCPD. Witness 102 explained that he came forward because he "felt bad about the situation," and he wanted to "bring closure to [Brown's] family," so they would not think that the officer "got away with murdering their son." He further explained that "most people think that police are bad for 'em up until the time they're in need of the police," and he felt that witnesses would not come forward to tell the truth in this case because of community pressure.

As described above, all of Witness 102's statements were materially consistent with each other, with physical and forensic evidence, and with other credible witness accounts. Witness 102 does not have a criminal history. Therefore, if called as a defense witness in a prosecution of Darren Wilson, this witness's account would not be vulnerable to meaningful cross-examination and would not be subject to impeachment due to bias or inconsistencies in his prior statements. Accordingly, after a thorough review of all the evidence, federal prosecutors

---

[23] As detailed below, the Monte Carlo in question was white.

determined his account to be credible and likewise determined that a jury appropriately would credit his potential testimony.

b. **Witness 103**

Witness 103 is a 58-year-old black male who gave two statements. First, Witness 103 was reluctant to meet with SLCPD detectives, FBI agents, and federal prosecutors because he has no particular allegiance to law enforcement. Witness 103 is a convicted felon who served time in federal prison, and has a son who was shot and injured by law enforcement during the commission of a robbery. Witness 103 expressed concerns because there were signs in the neighborhood of Canfield Drive stating, "snitches get stitches." Therefore, he agreed to be interviewed only on the condition of confidentiality. Witness 103 later testified before the county grand jury.

According to Witness 103, he was driving his blue pickup truck in the opposite direction of Wilson's SUV, and ended up virtually next to the driver's side of the SUV when it stopped. Relative to Witness 102, Witness 103 had a similar, but much closer view of the driver's side of the SUV. If the parked SUV is viewed as dividing Canfield Drive in half, both Witness 102 and Witness 103 were on the same side, with a view of Brown's back as he ran from Wilson, and a view of Brown's front as he ran toward Wilson.

When Witness 103 stopped his truck on Canfield Drive, although he did not see what led up to it, he saw Brown punching Wilson at least three times in the facial area, through the open driver's window of the SUV. Witness 103 described Wilson and Brown as having hold of each other's shirts, but Brown was "getting in a couple of blows." Wilson was leaning back toward the passenger seat with his forearm up, in an effort to block the blows. Then Witness 103 heard a gunshot and Brown took off running. Wilson exited the SUV, appeared to be using his shoulder microphone to call into his radio, and chased Brown with his gun held low.

Witness 103 explained that Brown came to a stop near a car, put his hand down on the car, and turned around to face Wilson. Brown's hands were then down at his sides. Witness 103 did not see Brown's hands up. Wanting to leave, Witness 103 began to turn his car around in the opposite direction that Brown had been running when he heard additional shots. Witness 103 turned to his right, and saw Brown "moving fast" toward Wilson. Witness 103 then drove away.

Witness 103 had a passenger in his truck. Although Witness 103 tried to facilitate contact between federal and state authorities and the passenger, the passenger refused to identify himself or provide any information.

When Witness 103 was initially subpoenaed to testify before the county grand jury, he expressed even more reluctance than he did during his investigative interview, this time alleging memory loss. However, he ultimately testified consistently with his original account, with the physical and forensic evidence, and with other credible witness accounts. Therefore, if called as a defense witness in a federal prosecution of Darren Wilson, Witness 103 would be subject to limited impeachment for his two felony convictions, including a theft conviction, but his apparent antipathy toward law enforcement would bolster testimony that corroborates Wilson.

Accordingly, after a thorough review of all the evidence, federal prosecutors determined his account to be credible, and likewise determined that a jury appropriately would credit his potential testimony.

c. **Witness 104**

Witness 104 is a 26-year-old bi-racial female. Witness 104 gave three statements. SLCPD detectives interviewed her, federal prosecutors and agents interviewed her, and she testified before the county grand jury.

Witness 104 was in a minivan that had been traveling in the opposite direction of Wilson, and came to a halt in front of Wilson's SUV, and somewhat behind, yet adjacent to Witness 103's blue pickup truck. Witness 104 was on the same side of the SUV as Witness 102 and Witness 103. She was seated in the middle row behind the driver's seat of the minivan, leaning over toward the center, with a direct view of Brown running away from Wilson, a frontal view of Brown coming back toward Wilson, and the shooting thereafter. Witness 104 is the adult daughter of the two witnesses in the driver and passenger front seats, Witness 105 and Witness 106, respectively. She is the sister of Witness 107, who was seated in the middle row passenger seat to her right.

According to Witness 104, she was leaning over, talking to her sister, Witness 107, when she heard two gunshots. She looked out the front window and saw Brown at the driver's window of Wilson's SUV. Witness 104 knew that Brown's arms were inside the SUV, but she could not see what Brown and Wilson were doing because Brown's body was blocking her view. Witness 104 saw Brown run from the SUV, followed by Wilson, who "hopped" out of the SUV and ran after him while yelling "stop, stop, stop." Wilson did not fire his gun as Brown ran from him. Brown then turned around and "for a second" began to raise his hands as though he may have considered surrendering, but then quickly "balled up in fists" in a running position and "charged" at Wilson. Witness 104 described it as a "tackle run," explaining that Brown "wasn't going to stop." Wilson fired his gun only as Brown charged at him, backing up as Brown came toward him. Witness 104 explained that there were three separate volleys of shots. Each time, Brown ran toward Wilson, Wilson fired, Brown paused, Wilson stopped firing, and then Brown charged again. The pattern continued until Brown fell to the ground, "smashing" his face upon impact. Wilson did not fire while Brown momentarily had his hands up. Witness 104 explained that it took some time for Wilson to fire, adding that she "would have fired sooner." Wilson did not go near Brown's body after Brown fell to his death.

Witness 104 explained that she first saw Brown's friend, Witness 101, when he took off running as soon as the first two shots were fired. She never saw him again.

All three of Witness 104's statements were consistent with each other, consistent with the physical and forensic evidence, and consistent with other credible witness accounts. Witness 104 does not have a criminal history. Therefore, if called as a defense witness in a prosecution of Darren Wilson, this witness's account would not be vulnerable to meaningful cross–examination and would not be subject to impeachment due to bias or inconsistencies in prior statements. Accordingly, after a thorough review of all the evidence, federal prosecutors determined her account to be credible, and likewise determined that a jury appropriately would credit her potential testimony.

d. **Witness 105**

Witness 105 is a 50-year-old black female. She gave two statements. SLCPD detectives interviewed her, and federal prosecutors explained the nature of the two parallel criminal investigations to Witness 105 prior to her testimony before the county grand jury. Witness 105 was driving a minivan in which Witness 104, her daughter, was seated behind the driver's seat in the middle row. Her husband, Witness 106, was next to her in the front passenger seat, and her other daughter, Witness 107, was seated behind her husband and next to Witness 104. Witness 105 had been traveling east on Canfield Drive, when she stopped in front of Wilson's vehicle with a view of the driver's side of his vehicle. Her view was also of the back of Brown as he first ran away, and then the front of Brown as he turned around and came back toward Wilson.

According to Witness 105, Wilson was driving a car, not an SUV, and a gunshot drew her attention to the vehicle. She noticed Brown's hands on Wilson's "car." Brown then ran eastbound and Wilson chased after him, gun in hand but held low. Witness 105 explained that Brown put his hands up "for a brief moment," and then turned around and made a shuffling movement. Wilson told Brown to "get down," but Brown did not comply. Instead, Brown put his hands down "in a running position." Witness 105 could not tell whether Brown was "charging" at Wilson or whether his plan was to run past Wilson, but either way, Brown was running toward Wilson. According to Witness 105, Wilson only shot at Brown when Brown was moving toward him. She could not see Brown's hands as he was running, but saw him reaching down as he began to fall to the ground. Witness 105 saw Wilson shoot Brown in the face before he began to stumble. Once Brown was on the ground, it appeared to Witness 105 that Wilson was calling out on the radio using his shoulder microphone.

When Witness 105 contacted SLCPD detectives, she was reluctant to identify herself and ultimately met with them in a library parking lot. She explained that she was coming forward because in speaking with her neighbors, she realized that what they believed had happened was inconsistent with what actually happened. She further explained that that she had not been paying attention to media accounts, and had been unaware of the inaccuracies being reported.

Both of Witness 105's statements were consistent with each other, materially consistent with the physical and forensic evidence, and consistent with other credible witness accounts in all material ways. Witness 105 has no criminal history. If called as a defense witness in a prosecution of Darren Wilson, this witness's account would be subject to limited impeachment on her ability to accurately perceive what occurred, e.g., that she perceived Wilson driving a car, rather than an SUV. However, that line of cross-examination does not undermine the overall consistency of her account with other credible witness accounts and with the physical evidence. Accordingly, after a thorough review of all the evidence, federal prosecutors determined her account to be largely credible and likewise determined that a jury appropriately would credit her potential testimony.

e. **Witness 108**

31

Witness 108 is a 74-year-old black male who claimed to have witnessed the shooting, stated that it was justified, but repeatedly refused to give formal statements to law enforcement for fear of reprisal should the Canfield Drive neighborhood find out that his account corroborated Wilson. He was served with a county grand jury subpoena and refused to appear.

During the initial canvass of the crime scene on August 9, 2014, in the hours after the shooting, SLCPD detectives approached Witness 108, who was sitting in his car on Canfield Drive. They asked if he witnessed what happened. Witness 108 refused to identify himself or give details, but told detectives that the police officer was "in the right" and "did what he had to do," and the statements made by people in the apartment complex were inaccurate. Both state and federal investigators later attempted to locate and interview Witness 108, who repeatedly expressed fear in coming forward. During the investigators' attempts to find Witness 108, another individual reported that two days after the shooting, Witness 108 confided in her that he "would have fucking shot that boy, too." In saying so, Witness 108 mimicked an aggressive stance with his hands out in front of him, as though he was about to charge. SLCPD detectives finally tracked down Witness 108 at a local repair shop, where he reluctantly explained that Wilson told Brown to "stop" or "get down" at least ten times, but instead Brown "charged" at Wilson. Witness 108 told detectives that there were other witnesses on Canfield Drive who witnessed the same thing. An SLCPD detective and federal prosecutor again tracked down Witness 108 in hopes of obtaining a more formal statement. However, Witness 108 refused to provide additional details to either county or federal authorities, citing community sentiment to support a "hands up" surrender narrative as his reason to remain silent. He explained that he would rather go to jail than testify before the county grand jury.

Witness 108 has no criminal history. Witness 108's accounts, although quite general, are clearly exculpatory as to Wilson and consistent with other credible evidence. His reluctance to testify in opposition to community sentiment lends further credence to his account.

f. **Witness 109**

Witness 109 is a 53 year-old black male. Like Witness 108, Witness 109 claimed to have witnessed the shooting, stated that it was justified, and repeatedly refused to give formal statements to law enforcement for fear of reprisal should the Canfield Drive neighborhood find out that his account corroborated Wilson. He was served with a county grand jury subpoena and refused to appear. Likewise, Witness 109 repeatedly refused to formally meet with SLCPD detectives, FBI agents, or federal and county prosecutors.

Law enforcement identified Witness 109 through a phone call that he made to the SLCPD information line at 5:19 p.m. on the day of the shooting. During that six-minute recorded call, the operator transferred Witness 109 to an SLCPD detective, and Witness 109 provided the following information, repeatedly refusing to meet with detectives in person. Witness 109 stated that he did not want his phone number traced, and would deny everything if it was traced. Witness 109 stated that he did not know Brown or his friend, Witness 101. However, he was calling because Witness 101, whom he described as the "guy with the dreads," lied on national television. Witness 109 described Brown and Witness 101 walking on the center line of the street when the officer asked them to get out of street. Brown responded something to the effect of, "Fuck the police." According to Witness 109, Wilson got out of his vehicle and Brown, the "young guy that died," hit him in the face. Witness 109 explained that Wilson reached for what appeared to be a taser but dropped it, and then grabbed a gun. Witness 109 explained that Brown reached for Wilson's gun. Although Witness 109's description was somewhat disjointed, he also stated that at first Brown ran away from Wilson, but then kept coming toward Wilson. Wilson told Brown to stop and lie down, but Brown failed to comply. Witness 109 said that Wilson fired in self-defense, explaining that Wilson did not shoot to kill at first, but "he unloaded on him when [Brown] wouldn't stop." Witness 109 said that "a lot of people saw that it was justified," ending the call by stating, "I know police get a bad rap, but they're here to protect us."

Federal and county prosecutors and investigators tried to no avail to interview Witness 109. True to his word on that initial phone call, he would not discuss what he saw. He did, however, acknowledge that he placed a call to the SLCPD information line.

Witness 109 does have a criminal history that would be admissible in federal court. Witness 109 has a misdemeanor theft conviction from 1985 and a felony arrest, both of which likely would be inadmissible in federal court for impeachment purposes. Witness 109's account is exculpatory as to Wilson and although Witness 109 may be subject to limited impeachment, the majority of his description is consistent with the physical and forensic evidence, and consistent with other credible witness accounts. Community sentiment and therefore his reluctance to testify on behalf of Wilson would likely bolster his account.

g. **Witness 113**

Witness 113 is a 31-year-old black female. She was interviewed one time by FBI agents during their canvass on August 16, 2014, and gave an account that generally corroborated Wilson, but only after she was confronted with untruthful statements she initially made in an effort to avoid neighborhood backlash. When local authorities tried to serve Witness 113 with a subpoena to testify before the county grand jury, she blockaded her door with a couch to avoid service.

Witness 113 was on her brother's balcony, located opposite and to the left of the aforementioned minivan, when she first saw Brown walking in the street. Contrary to other witness accounts, Witness 113 saw what she believed to be three black males walking in the street, and two police vehicles present, calling into question whether she actually witnessed the beginning of the incident. She explained that one of the police officers told Brown and his friends to go on the sidewalk, and then subsequently called Brown over to his vehicle, where a struggle occurred.

Witness 113 then gave an account that was contrary to physical evidence, internally inconsistent, and admittedly untrue. She first explained that Brown ran east, away from Wilson, as Wilson shot at him. However, she then explained that she watched as Brown ran west past Wilson, who shot Brown right next to the SUV. Witness 113 stated that Wilson fired shots into Brown's back as he lay flat on his stomach on the ground. When the FBI told Witness 113 that the autopsy results and other evidence were inconsistent with her account, she admitted that she lied. She explained to the FBI that, "You've gotta live the life to know it," and stated that she feared offering an account contrary to the narrative reported by the media that Brown held his hands up in surrender.

Witness 113 then admitted that she saw Brown running toward Wilson, prompting Wilson to yell, "Freeze." Brown failed to stop and Wilson began shooting Brown. Witness 113 told the FBI that it appeared to her that Wilson's life was in danger. She explained there was a pause in the shots before the firing resumed, but Witness 113 had ducked down for cover and did not see anything after the first volley of shots.

Witness 113 was with her brother and boyfriend when the shooting occurred. Witness 113 refused to provide their contact information, and they both repeatedly evaded law enforcement's attempts to meet with them.

Witness 113 has no criminal history that would be admissible in federal court. Witness 113 has past arrests but no convictions, which likely would be inadmissible in federal court. In a federal prosecution, if served and called to testify on behalf of Wilson, federal prosecutors could subject Witness 113 to cross-examination due to her admittedly untruthful statements during the first part of her interview with the FBI. However, her reasons for being untruthful, coupled with the fact that she immediately changed course when her statements were challenged, give her account reliability. Accordingly, prosecutors did not discount her narrative in its entirety, but rather in examining all of the evidence, considered this witness's account in making a prosecutive decision.

h. **Witness 134**

Witness 134 is a 36-year-old white female. She was interviewed one time by federal authorities. At the time of her interview with federal agents and prosecutors, she was Wilson's fiancée and was Wilson's field training officer in 2011. Prosecutors considered her potential bias when interviewing Witness 134, but sought out and evaluated her account for several reasons. First, as noted below in the legal analysis, to make a determination as to whether a potential civil rights defendant has the requisite criminal intent, prosecutors must consider a subject officer's training as part of an evaluation of his overall understanding of when the use of deadly force is permissible. Second, Witness 134 spoke to Wilson minutes after the shooting, while he was arguably still under the stress of the situation and immediately after he perceived it. It is possible that in a prosecution of Wilson, defense counsel would be permitted to introduce Wilson's initial statements to Witness 134 through the "present sense impression" or "excited utterance" hearsay exceptions. Fed. R. Evid. 803(1); 803(2).

Witness 134 explained that when she was Wilson's field training officer for the FPD, he did not require a lot of training because he had prior experience as a law enforcement officer. Wilson knew and understood that he was permitted to use physical force when he or someone else was met with a physical threat. As Wilson's training officer, she never had concerns as to whether he understood when he was permitted to use force.

Witness 134 was on light duty on August 9, 2014, working at the police department building because she was pregnant. She was working the same shift as Wilson and was waiting to join him for lunch. Witness 134 stated that when Wilson arrived at the FPD at about 12:15 p.m., he did not seem like himself. His face was red and puffy, consistent with injury. Knowing something was wrong, she asked Wilson what happened. Wilson responded, "I just killed someone." Wilson also told her that he had washed blood from his hands.

Witness 134 also explained that other than facial injuries, she did not notice additional injuries or blood on Wilson, but she did notice blood on the hammer of his gun, still holstered in his belt. Wilson asked her to retrieve latex gloves for him, which Wilson then used to clear and package his gun. Witness 134 did not actually see Wilson do this because her back was to him, although she could hear what he was doing. She also saw the envelope, presumably containing the gun, sealed with evidence tape, but did not know who eventually took it to an evidence locker.

Prior to packaging his gun, Wilson gave Witness 134 a narrative consistent with the accounts he later gave throughout the course of the investigation. Federal agents and prosecutors asked Witness 134 to be specific about what Wilson told her at the police department in the immediate aftermath as opposed to subsequent conversations that they have had since the shooting. Witness 134 was certain that Wilson told her the following: He told Brown and his friend to get out of the street, but did not say anything "ignorant" that would anger them. As Wilson was passing Brown and his friend, he saw cigarillos in Brown's hand and noticed Witness 101's black shirt and realized that they matched the description of the suspects involved in the "stealing in progress." As Brown was attacking Wilson, Wilson explained that in his mind, he went through the weapons available to him on his gun belt. He knew that he had no choice but to use his gun.

Wilson explained to Witness 134 that he was able to shoot inside the SUV, but did not know where the bullet went and whether it hit Brown. Brown ran off and Wilson chased him, explaining to Witness 134 that "all of a sudden," Brown stopped, turned around, and started "charging" him. Witness 134 explained that although she could not remember the exact words Wilson said he used, he said something like, "Get on the ground," trying to get Brown to stop. However, Wilson told her that Brown did not stop and continued to charge at Wilson. Wilson fired at Brown and continued to do so until Brown was on the ground because Brown "just wouldn't stop."

Witness 134 explained that Wilson was shaken, but confident that he did the right thing in the moment, although he became worried in the few minutes that followed the shooting because the neighborhood was quickly becoming hostile.

Witness 134 explained that in all of their conversations, Wilson had been adamant that Brown's hands were not up, but rather, Brown's right hand was in his waistband with his left hand in a fist, as though he was running. Witness 134 said that she was relieved to see the results of the private autopsy in the media because it showed a series of shots in Brown's right arm, consistent with Wilson's explanation that he had tunnel vision during the shooting.

After learning of Witness 101's account alleging that Wilson grabbed Brown's throat by reaching out the driver's window and then subsequently shooting him while he was surrendering, Wilson told Witness 134 that Witness 101 was not present for the shooting because he saw Witness 101 run off as soon as Brown handed him the cigarillos during the assault at the SUV window. Wilson and Witness 134 agreed that the notion that a police officer would attempt to pull an individual into his vehicle, especially someone as big as Brown, is contrary to training. Wilson described Brown as Hulk Hogan-like, such that he could have easily overpowered Wilson.

Witness 134 has no criminal history. If called as a defense witness in a prosecution of Darren Wilson, Witness 134 would be subject to cross- examination due to obvious bias. However, her account of what Wilson told her is consistent with Wilson's previous statements, with other credible witness accounts, and with the forensic and physical evidence. Accordingly, having met Witness 134 and considered her manner and demeanor, federal prosecutors found her account credible. Nonetheless, because of Witness 134's relationship with Wilson and because most of her information came directly from Wilson, prosecutors did not heavily rely on her account when making a prosecutive decision.

> ii. *Witnesses Consistent with Prior Statements, Physical Evidence, and Other Witnesses Who Inculpate Wilson*

There are no witnesses who fall under this category.

> 2. Witnesses Who Neither Inculpate Nor Fully Corroborate Wilson

> i. **Witness 107**

Witness 107 is a 30-year-old black female. Witness 107 was seated in the passenger seat in the middle row of a minivan that was stopped opposite Wilson's SUV at the time of the shooting. Witness 107 was seated next to her sister Witness 104 and behind her father, Witness 106. Witness 105, her mother, was seated in the driver's seat. However, when Witness 107 initially described what happened, she mistakenly thought she was in the front passenger seat and forgot that her father was present. She also mistakenly thought that they had been driving in the same direction as Wilson.

Witness 107 gave three statements. First, an SLCPD detective and an FBI agent jointly interviewed her. Federal prosecutors and agents conducted a follow-up interview to address inconsistencies with the physical evidence in her original account. Witness 107 also testified before the county grand jury.

According to Witness 107, she was looking at her mobile phone when she heard two gunshots. She looked up and out the front windshield, and saw Brown run away from Wilson. Witness 107 mistakenly thought that Wilson was standing toward the front of the passenger side of the police vehicle, and could not remember whether the vehicle was an SUV or a car. Wilson then chased after Brown and drew his gun, shooting three times. Contrary to the autopsy results, Witness 107 stated that Wilson shot Brown in the leg and hip as Brown was running away.

Brown then turned around and briefly put his hands with up, palms forward, near his shoulders, as though he was "giving up." But then Brown put his hands down, one of them holding his chest, as he came back toward Wilson, though Witness 107 was unsure whether Brown was stumbling or running. Wilson fired the last shots from 10 to 15 feet away from Brown, and kept shooting as Brown was falling to the ground.

Witness 107 explained that immediately following the shooting, her mother drove to a nearby parking lot. She and her family members discussed what they witnessed, and they all seemed to have witnessed different things. Her sister, Witness 104, for example, was adamant that Brown "charged" at Wilson, whereas Witness 107 expressed uncertainty. The family also could not reach a consensus as to the number of shots fired.

When Witness 107 met with federal prosecutors and agents, she was visibly shaken by what she witnessed, articulating the difficulty of watching someone die. However, given the differences among what she and her family saw, and realizing that she was factually incorrect about the direction of the police vehicle, the location where Wilson stood, and where the bullets struck Brown, she was not certain about what she believed she witnessed.

Witness 107 has one prior misdemeanor arrest that likely would not be admissible in federal court. As detailed above, Witness 107 was admittedly mistaken or unsure about some of what she perceived, rendering her account vulnerable to effective cross-examination. Regardless of credibility, her account does not inculpate Darren Wilson and does not support a federal prosecution.

ii. **Witness 106**

Witness 106 is a 45-year-old white male. As mentioned, he was seated in the front passenger seat of a minivan, driven by his wife, Witness 105. Witness 106's daughters, Witness 104 and Witness 107, were seated in the middle row of the minivan, behind the driver and front seat passenger, respectively. According to Witness 106, although his wife saw Wilson emerge from what she remembered was a police car, he first saw Wilson and Brown when they were in the street. It initially looked to Witness 106 like Brown had a gun and there was a firefight happening, although he has since realized that not to be the case. Regardless, Witness 106's overall impression was that he witnessed a police officer "taking down a gunman in a residential neighborhood before anyone else got hurt." It was for that reason that Witness 106 agreed to speak with SLCPD detectives. He otherwise does not "have any love" for law enforcement, having served 18 years in prison. Witness 106 also testified before the county grand jury.

Witness 106 explained that he first saw Brown as he ran from Wilson. Wilson fired one shot which seemed to hit Brown in the leg because Brown appeared to stagger. Brown's arms then "briefly flung" out and he turned around to face Wilson. Witness 106 then explained that even though the neighborhood had been talking about Brown having his "hands up," Brown "did not have his hands up." Brown's arms were down at his sides, such that Witness 106 could not even see Brown's hands. Witness 106's vantage point was over Wilson's shoulder. Witness 106 saw Brown walk toward Wilson and thought that Brown was about to shoot Wilson, as Wilson shot Brown until he fell to his death. Wilson was about six to 10 feet from Brown when he fired the final shots at Brown.

Witness 106's account is inconsistent with the physical and forensic evidence and other credible witness accounts. He has a conviction for sexual abuse that would likely be admissible in federal court as impeachment evidence, although his bias tends to bolster his account. Regardless of its credibility, Witness 106's account does not inculpate Darren Wilson and therefore does not support a federal prosecution.

iii. **Witness 110**

Witness 110 is a 51-year-old black male who is married to Witness 111. Witness 110 spoke to SLCPD detectives on two occasions. As noted below, the second interview occurred because Witness 111 was too upset to complete the first interview. Witness 110 also testified before the county grand jury.

Witness 110 and Witness 111 first came into contact with SLCPD detectives because they were attending a social function the evening of August 9, 2014. The couple told a friend, an attorney, what they had witnessed, and the friend called the SLCPD on their behalf. SLCPD detectives responded to the venue of the social function to interview Witness 110 and Witness 111, but they were reluctant to speak to law enforcement, fearing retaliation from people in the community. They agreed to speak only on the condition of confidentiality. However, during that initial contact with SLCPD detectives, Witness 111 began crying and could not talk about what she witnessed. Witness 110 was too shaken to give a full account, but he did explain that earlier that day, he and his wife were at the Canfield Green Apartments complex visiting Witness 110's elderly mother and brother, Witness 112. He then gave a brief account which he detailed a few days later when he met again with SLCPD detectives.

According to Witness 110, he and Witness 111 were driving on Canfield Drive when they noticed Brown and his friend, Witness 101, walking in the center of the street and had to veer around them to avoid hitting them. Witness 111 commented to Witness 110, "Why don't they just get on the sidewalk?" As they were pulling into the driveway of the building they were visiting, they noticed Wilson driving in the opposite direction. During his initial interview with SLCPD detectives, Witness 110 explained that while in the driveway, he noticed Brown standing beside the driver's door of the SUV, with the upper portion of his body inside the driver's area of the SUV. Witness 110 did not mention this during his second interview with SLCPD detectives or when he testified in front of the county grand jury.

Witness 110 then explained that he and Witness 111 went up to the second floor apartment balcony, located opposite and off to the right of the minivan with Witness 104, Witness 105, Witness 106, and Witness 107. Their vantage point was of the passenger side of the SUV, followed by the right profile of Brown as he ran away from Wilson, and then the left profile of Brown as he turned around and moved toward Wilson.

Witness 110 stated that he witnessed an exchange between Wilson, Brown, and Witness 101, but did not hear what was said. Wilson reversed his vehicle, using it to block Brown and Witness 101. Brown and Wilson engaged in a back and forth "scuffle," although Witness 110 could not see exactly what happened because the SUV blocked his view of Brown. They then heard a shot and Witness 101 "disappeared." Brown remained at the SUV and the scuffle continued until there was a second gunshot and Brown took off running. When Brown reached a nearby driveway, he stopped and looked down at his hand, which Witness 111 noted had blood on it. Witness 110 believed that Brown looked at his left hand. Brown put his hands out at his sides, palms up, as though asking, "What the heck?" Brown then moved toward Wilson with his hands in that same position, and Wilson shot Brown. Brown then paused, the shooting stopped, and then Brown advanced again. Witness 110 stated that Wilson shot Brown only when Brown was moving toward him, and did not shoot at Brown as he ran away. Witness 110 initially told SLCPD detectives that Brown moved "quickly," although he testified in the county grand jury that he could not describe how Brown was moving toward Wilson, though he was not "charging" or "running." At no time were Brown's hands up in surrender or otherwise.

Witness 110 has no criminal history. As noted, Witness 110's second interview was consistent with his grand jury testimony, though partially inconsistent with what he initially told SLCPD detectives. Nonetheless, Witness 110's account was consistent with the physical and forensic evidence. Regardless of the credibility of his account, it does not inculpate Wilson, and therefore does not support a federal prosecution.

iv. **Witness 111**

Witness 111 is a 48-year-old black female who is married to Witness 110. As mentioned, she was too upset to speak with SLCPD detectives on the evening of August 9, 2014, but did speak to law enforcement on August 18, 2014, when she was jointly interviewed by SLCPD detectives, FBI agents, and federal prosecutors. Federal authorities also met with Witness 110 at that time. Witness 111 subsequently testified before the county grand jury.

Witness 111's account is consistent with the account of Witness 110, with two exceptions. First, when she witnessed Brown turn around after fleeing from Wilson, Witness 111 explained that Brown looked down at his right hand, which was bleeding. This is contrary to Witness 110, who said that Brown looked down at his left hand and did not mention seeing blood. Second, Witness 111 described Brown as moving back toward Wilson in "slow motion," where Witness 110 at one time described Brown walking "quickly," but later could not characterize his pace. According to Witness 111, at no time were Brown's hands up in surrender or otherwise.

Witness 111 has no criminal history. Witness 111's statements were consistent with each other, and with the physical and forensic evidence, and therefore, Witness 111 would not be vulnerable to cross-examination on those grounds. However, Witness 111 was especially distraught during her investigatory interview, stating that she, too, has a teenage son and commenting that she wished Wilson had used a form of less lethal force. Her bias could subject her to effective cross-examination, and led federal prosecutors to question whether her bias was affecting her ability to accurately recall events. Regardless, Witness 111's account does not inculpate Wilson, and therefore does not support a federal prosecution.

v. **Witness 115**

Witness 115 is a 32-year-old black male. Witness 115 gave three investigatory statements and was interviewed by the media on several occasions. First, SLCPD detectives interviewed Witness 115 within hours of Brown's death. Second, federal agents and prosecutors conducted a follow-up interview, during which they challenged Witness 115 on what he actually witnessed as opposed to what he assumed had taken place. Witness 115 also testified before the county grand jury.

According to Witness 115, he was in his second floor apartment at the time of the shooting, on the same side of the SUV as the minivan occupied by Witness 104, Witness 105, Witness 106, and Witness 107, but with a view of Brown's right profile as he was coming back toward Wilson. Just before noon, Witness 115 was in his bedroom when he heard what he thought was an altercation. He described hearing "strong voices" or loud grunts, but could not make out specific words or sounds. Witness 115 went to his window and looked through horizontal blinds by pushing them apart. He saw Brown at the driver's door of the SUV and "arms were being exchanged." Federal prosecutors and agents asked Witness 115 to demonstrate Brown's actions, and he did so by making a fist and a punching motion. Witness 115 demonstrated that Wilson had his arm bent across his chest in a defensive position, but he was reluctant to state that Brown "punched" Wilson. However, after federal prosecutors played Witness 115's own cell phone video back to him, he acknowledged that on the video, recorded right after Brown died, he narrated, "Dude was all up in his car; dude was punching on him," and that "dude" was Brown. Witness 115 explained that his initial impression was that Brown was punching Wilson because Brown was on the outside, standing on the street, and appeared to have the upper hand.

Witness 115 explained that he suddenly saw both Brown and his friend, Witness 101, who had been standing toward the front part of the SUV, start running. Witness 115 did not know why they started to run and he did not hear a gunshot, though he acknowledged that the suddenness with which they ran was consistent with a shot being fired. Brown ran down the middle of the street and Witness 101 started to crouch down by a white Monte Carlo. According to Witness 115, Wilson then got out of his SUV, gun drawn, and immediately fired shots as he began to quickly walk in Brown's direction. With each shot, Witness 101 ducked down a little more, creeping around the Monte Carlo until he went from the driver's side to the passenger side, and out of Witness 115's view. Witness 115 explained that while he was watching Witness 101, he was not watching Brown, who had disappeared from his range of view once he ran from Wilson.

Witness 115 stated that there was a pause in the shooting and he used this opportunity to go out on his balcony to get a better look. As he did, he realized that he left his mobile phone on his dresser. He went back to his bedroom, retrieved his phone, and returned to his balcony. At the same time, he called to his wife, Witness 124, who joined him with their three children. By the time Witness 115 saw Brown again, Brown was walking back toward Wilson with his arms folded across his stomach. Witness 115 said he "assumed" that Wilson had shot Brown in the stomach, although he did not see this happen. This assumption is inconsistent with the autopsy findings.

Witness 115 stated that he did not see Brown with his hands up and Brown did not appear to be surrendering. Rather, Brown looked as though he was slowly going down to the ground as he walked toward Wilson. Wilson then fired another volley of shots and Brown fell to the ground with one arm under him and the other at his side. Consistent with Wilson's account, Witness 115 explained that once Brown was on the ground, Wilson kept his gun drawn and appeared to be talking in his radio on his shoulder. According to Witness 115, at no time did Wilson touch Brown's body.

Witness 115 described the crowds that began to form immediately after the shooting, as people began to gather and talk about what happened. Witness 115 explained that although he initially spoke to SLCPD detectives only four hours after the incident, by then, he had already discussed the incident with Witness 124 and with a passerby on the street. He explained that this passerby can be heard on Witness 115's cell phone video, attempting to correct Witness 115, as Witness 115 narrated that Brown had been punching Wilson.

Witness 115 expressed that he felt comfortable with federal prosecutors and agents who were questioning him about assumptions and inconsistencies. However, Witness 115 was concerned that because of the constant talk in the neighborhood and his multiple media appearances without the presence of a lawyer, he may have unwittingly made inconsistent statements in the past.

Witness 115 has one prior misdemeanor conviction, which likely would be inadmissible in federal court as impeachment evidence. Witness 115 is vulnerable to effective cross-examination because he did not witness significant parts of the shooting and based parts of his account on assumption. Regardless of credibility, Witness 115's account does not inculpate Darren Wilson and therefore does not support a federal prosecution.

vi. **Witness 141**

Witness 141 is a 19-year-old black male who moved out of Missouri after the shooting. Witness 141 gave three statements. First, FBI agents based in Texas interviewed him. Federal prosecutors and agents conducted a follow-up interview. Finally, Witness 141 testified before the county grand jury.

According to Witness 141, he was sitting on his balcony when he saw Brown and Witness 101 walking down the middle of Canfield Drive. Witness 141 knew Brown through a friend, but did not have regular interaction with him. Unrelated to the shooting incident, Witness 141 went into his apartment to retrieve his mobile phone. While inside, he heard gunshots, prompting him to go back out to the balcony. Witness 141 saw Wilson pointing his gun at Brown, who had his hand across his front torso or waist. Brown never had his hands up in surrender or otherwise. Brown appeared to be stumbling or walking toward Wilson, who fired about five to seven shots at Brown from a distance of about eight feet. Brown collapsed to the ground. Witness 141 did not see Witness 101 anywhere. Witness 141 used his mobile phone to record a video in the aftermath of Brown's death.

Witness 141 testified before the county grand jury that he thought that after Wilson fired the first shot, the additional shots were "excessive," an opinion that would be inadmissible in federal court, and a misstatement of the applicable federal law. Witness 141 based that opinion on the fact that he did not perceive Brown to be a physical threat. However, he acknowledged that he did not see what led up to the initial shots, and did not see Brown run from Wilson, turn around to face Wilson, or any of Brown's actions during that time. Rather, he only saw Wilson shoot Brown as Brown moved toward him.

Witness 141 has no criminal history. Witness 141's statements were consistent with each other, but he did not witness large parts of the incident. Regardless of whether his account is credible, it does not inculpate Darren Wilson and therefore does not support a federal prosecution.

vii.   **Witness 114**

Witness 114 is a 75-year-old black female. She gave two statements. First, she was interviewed by the FBI, and she later testified before the county grand jury.

Witness 114 saw the initial interaction between Brown and Wilson from her second floor window. Witness 114's view was of the passenger side of Wilson's SUV. Witness 114 saw Brown and Witness 101 walking in the middle of Canfield Drive, when Wilson stopped his SUV and leaned his head out of the driver's window as though saying something to Brown. Brown then made some sort of hand gesture, indicating to Witness 114 that he was responding to Wilson. Wilson continued driving, but then jerked back his SUV and parked it at an angle, with the back of the SUV closer to the center of the street. According to Witness 114, Brown remained there, while Witness 101 kept walking. She did not see Witness 101 again.

Next, Witness 114 saw Wilson hold onto Brown, though she was unsure how the physical contact began. Witness 114 stated that Wilson and Brown were "tussling," explaining that she could see Brown's hands inside the SUV by looking through the passenger side window. However, she did not see any other part of his body go into the SUV because Brown was standing straight up. From her perspective, it looked like Brown was trying to pull away. Yet Witness 114 acknowledged that had Wilson un-holstered his gun in the manner he described, it was also possible, given Brown's position, that Brown reached for Wilson's gun.

Witness 114 watched Brown run from the SUV, followed by Wilson with his gun drawn, until they both disappeared from her line of sight. She heard two gunshots followed by six more gunshots, but did not see Wilson fire any shots. Witness 114 changed her clothes and went down to street level to see Brown's body in the street.

Witness 114 has no criminal history. Witness 114's statements were consistent with each other, however, she did not see the majority of the shooting. Accordingly, her account does not inculpate Wilson and therefore does not support a federal prosecution.

viii.   **Witness 129**

Witness 129 is a 22-year-old black male. He gave two statements. First, FBI agents interviewed him as part of their canvass on August 16, 2014. Second, Witness 129 testified before the county grand jury.

Witness 129 was outside his apartment when he saw Brown and his friend, Witness 101, walking in the middle of Canfield Drive. Wilson pulled up next to them in his SUV. Brown and Witness 101 kept walking and Wilson backed up to cut them off. Brown and Wilson then engaged in a "scuffle." Witness 129's view was of the passenger side of the SUV. Therefore, although he could tell that Wilson remained in the driver's seat of the SUV while Brown was standing outside of the SUV, Witness 129 could not describe exactly what Brown and Wilson were doing or how the upper half of Brown's body was positioned relative to the SUV. Witness 129 then heard a gunshot, but Brown remained at the SUV and the scuffle continued for another 20 to 30 seconds. A second shot then went off and Brown ran eastbound down Canfield Drive. Witness 129 explained that Witness 101 ducked behind a white car, ran around it, and went in the other direction. Wilson got out of the SUV and fired one or two shots, though Witness 129 did not see whether the shots struck Brown, nor did he see what Brown was doing, because a nearby building blocked his view.

Witness 129 has no criminal history. Witness 129's statements were materially consistent with each other and consistent with other credible evidence. However, Witness 129's account does not inculpate Wilson, and therefore does not support a federal prosecution.

ix. **Witness 116**

Witness 116 is a 16-year-old black male. He gave three statements. First, he met with SLCPD detectives within hours of the shooting in the presence of his father and father's girlfriend. He subsequently met with federal agents and prosecutors. Finally, he testified before the county grand jury.

Witness 116 explained that he was in his apartment watching television when he heard screams, prompting him to go to the window and look out of the vertical blinds. Witness 116 saw Brown with his hands inside the driver's side of the SUV. He then saw Wilson take out what appeared to be a taser. Wilson shot the taser one time, but missed, which is why Witness 116 surmised that Wilson took out his gun. Brown's friend, Witness 101, took off running somewhere into the apartment complexes.

Wilson shot once or twice, and Brown, with arms at his sides, ran out of view. Witness 116 looked away because he assumed that Brown had been apprehended. He then heard five or six more shots and looked back out the window to see Brown dead on the ground. Witness 116 did not see what happened leading up to Brown standing by the SUV.

Witness 116's statements were consistent, but he also mistakenly believed that Wilson used a taser. Regardless of the reliability of his account, Witness 116 did not witness significant parts of the shooting. Like several of the witnesses in this section of the report, that which he did see does not inculpate Darren Wilson and therefore does not support a federal prosecution.

3. Witnesses Whose Accounts Do Not Support a Prosecution Due to Materially Inconsistent Prior Statements or Inconsistencies With the Physical and Forensic Evidence

i. **Witness 101**

Witness 101 is a 22-year-old black male who was walking in the middle of Canfield Drive with Brown when they encountered Wilson. Witness 101 made multiple statements to the media immediately following the incident that spawned the popular narrative that Wilson shot Brown execution-style as he held up his hands in surrender. These media interviews occurred prior to Witness 101 giving his two statements. First, FBI and SLCPD jointly interviewed Witness 101 on August 13, 2014, in the presence of Witness 101's mother, Witness 101's two attorneys, and an individual who explained that he was in charge of Witness 101's personal security. Witness 101 subsequently testified before the county grand jury.

According to Witness 101, he and Brown had been friends for about two to three months as of the day of the shooting. Witness 101 viewed himself as a role model or mentor to Brown. Witness 101 came into contact with Brown on August 9, 2014, at about 7:00 a.m. At some point between then and just prior to noon, he and Brown decided to go to Ferguson Market to get cigarillos. Witness 101 could not recall in detail what the pair was doing in those five intervening hours, other than to explain that they were playing video games and talking. However, Witness 101 explained that just prior to going to Ferguson Market, Brown engaged in a 25-minute conversation about marijuana with one of two contractors who were working in the apartment complex.

Witness 101 explained that when they went to Ferguson Market, Brown stole cigarillos from behind the counter as though he was entitled to them, and then subsequently shoved the store clerk, who was substantially smaller in stature than Brown, who was 6'5" and 289 lbs. Witness 101 initially minimized these events when speaking with law enforcement, but then acknowledged to the county grand jury that Brown was surprisingly aggressive. Brown's behavior caught Witness 101 off guard because it was uncharacteristic of Brown and contrary to Brown's usual behavior. Witness 101 expected to encounter the police when they left Ferguson Market because he heard the clerk say he was going to call the police. Witness 101 described Brown's behavior as "bold" when Brown openly carried the stolen cigarillos as they walked down Canfield Drive.

Witness 101 and Brown were walking eastbound, single-file, on Canfield Drive in the center of the street on the yellow line when they encountered Wilson driving in the opposite direction in his marked FPD SUV. Witness 101 explained that they had not been obstructing traffic, although several cars had to avoid Brown and Witness 101 as they drove by. Wilson told them to "get the fuck on the sidewalk," and Witness 101 responded that they were "not but one minute from their destination." Brown and Witness 101 did not move onto the sidewalk, but continued to walk in the middle of the street. As Wilson drove past them, he reversed his SUV and parked it at an angle, blocking both lanes in the road and almost hitting them, asking, "What did you just say?" According to Witness 101, Wilson attempted to open the driver's side in an "aggressive" and "forceful" manner. The door opened less than an inch because of Brown and

Witness 101's proximity to the door. The door quickly bounced off of Brown and Witness 101 and shut on Wilson. According to Witness 101, this angered Brown. Witness 101 also stated that he understood how Wilson could have perceived that Brown shut the door on him.

According to Witness 101, Wilson then reached out the window and up with his left hand, grabbing Brown by the throat. The private forensic pathologist termed such an action "surprising," based on the autopsy results and his experience as a forensic pathologist. Wilson and Brown engaged in a "tug of war," during which Wilson unsuccessfully tried to pull Brown toward the SUV as Brown attempted to pull away, while still holding the cigarillos. Witness 101 told county and federal investigators that Brown told Wilson, "Get the fuck off me. We're not doin' anything wrong. Leave us the fuck alone." However, Witness 101 explained that even though Wilson had his grip on Brown, Brown had the upper hand both because of his stature and his physical position relative to the car. As Witness 101 told investigators, Wilson would have to be "superhuman" to "overpower" Brown. Witness 101 told the county grand jury that Brown was getting "the best of the officer" because Wilson was only using his left hand. During this tug of war, Wilson's grip gradually slipped from Brown's throat to his shirt, down to his shoulder and arm. Although Witness 101 told the county grand jury that Wilson gripped Brown's right arm, Witness 101 told investigators that Wilson mostly was gripping Brown's shirt by pulling it down over Brown's forearm. According to Witness 101, at no point did Brown ever strike, punch, or grab any part of Wilson. He could offer no explanation as to how Wilson sustained injury, other than to speculate that it was the result of their "tug of war."

As the "tug of war" continued, Brown was then able to turn to his right toward Witness 101 and hand off the cigarillos with both hands. Brown then put his left hand on the door frame under the rearview mirror, while Wilson, using his left hand, maintained hold of Brown's right arm or sleeve. According to Witness 101, Wilson used his right hand to grab hold of Brown's left arm, although it is unclear from Witness 101's accounts whether he actually saw that happen or assumed it happened. Wilson, also using his right hand, then took out his gun and said, "I'm going to shoot." Witness 101 saw Wilson holding the gun and aiming it out the window when Wilson again started to say, "I'm going to shoot."

Witness 101 explained that Wilson fired, hitting Brown in the torso. Witness 101 described blood on the right side of Brown's torso. At the time of the shot, Brown was standing straight, his midsection up against the door, with his left hand down at his side and Wilson gripping Brown's right arm. Contrary to the autopsy results, particularly with regard to the thumb wound and the round recovered from the inside of the driver's door, Witness 101 was adamant that Wilson neither fired a shot within the SUV, nor did Brown have his hand(s) near the gun when the first shot was fired. Witness 101 explained that Wilson fired the shot and "the bullet traveled outside the car and struck [Brown] in the chest." Witness 101 was equally adamant that Brown's hands and arms never entered the SUV, telling investigators that the only hand that would have been "free" would have been Brown's left hand, and that hand neither entered the vehicle nor "reached for" Wilson's gun. However, when he testified before the county grand jury, Witness 101 made room for the possibility that Brown's arm entered the SUV when he was not looking.

According to Witness 101, after the first shot, Brown and Witness 101 simultaneously ran eastbound, away from the SUV. Witness 101 explained that he got ahead of Brown, such

45

that his back was to both Brown and Wilson. Fearing for his life, Witness 101 crouched down among the cars that had now stopped in the middle of the street because of the parked SUV. Witness 101 attempted to get into a nearby car, a gray Sunfire, but the occupants would not allow him inside. Brown ran past Witness 101, telling him, "Keep running, bro." After a pause, Witness 101 explained that he heard Wilson emerge from the SUV. Witness 101 stood up and watched "in plain sight" as Wilson passed him and chased after Brown.

According to Witness 101, Wilson then fired a second shot which appeared to strike Brown in the back. Brown's arms were not raised at that time. During his investigative interview, Witness 101 stated that the bullet "definitely struck [Brown] in the back." During his county grand jury testimony, Witness 101 stated that the bullet likely "grazed" Brown's arm, acknowledging that since he had made his original statements, he had watched media reports of the privately-commissioned autopsy of Brown. Witness 101 said that he assumed that had Brown not been struck, he would have kept on running. Instead, Brown stopped. Brown put his hands up above his head, in the air, and turned around to face Wilson. In so doing, one arm was lower than the other, though Witness 101 could not say whether it was the left or right arm. According to Witness 101, Brown then stated, "I don't have a gun" or "I'm unarmed." Brown started to say it again, but Wilson, while walking toward Brown, fired one volley of at least four shots and Brown fell to his death. Wilson never said a word; he never commanded Brown to stop or freeze. Witness 101 was steadfast that Brown fell to the ground right where he initially stopped and turned around. At most, Brown took a half-step forward, but he did not move toward Wilson. Witness 101 was also steadfast that Brown never put his hand(s) near his waist. As described earlier, the physical evidence establishes that Brown moved forward about 20 feet toward Wilson, and the SLCME medicolegal investigator found Brown with his left hand at his waistband.

Witness 101 also told the county grand jury that he "stood and watched face-to-face as every shot was fired as [Brown]'s body [fell] to the ground," but was unaware that Wilson shot Brown in the face and head until he saw media reports of the privately-commissioned autopsy. Until then, he thought the only shots were to Brown's "upper region" and chest.

Witness 101 ran from the scene, saying, "He just killed my friend." Witness 101 went home and changed his shirt, so he later would not be recognized by the police. By the time he went back to the scene of the shooting, the streets were crowded with people, but, contrary to the dispatch recordings and cellular phone video, there were no police officers on scene. When police officers did arrive, he did not want to speak with them. Instead, Witness 101 went to Brown's grandmother's home and told her and other family members what happened. With the encouragement of Brown's family, Witness 101 went back out onto the street and gave an interview to the media.

During his testimony before the county grand jury, Witness 101 acknowledged that he had discussed the incident with another witness, Witness 118. Witness 101 explained that he was friendly with Witness 118, and noticed her standing on her balcony when he and Brown first encountered Wilson on Canfield Drive. He explained that he was surprised that so many other witnesses came forward because Witness 118 was the only person he saw outside, and she was the only person who saw the incident from the "first shot to the last shot." However, as detailed below, Witness 118 was not out on her balcony for the majority of the incident, and it is unknown at what point she actually witnessed the shootings, if at all.

Witness 101 has a misdemeanor conviction for a crime of dishonesty likely admissible in federal court as impeachment evidence. As described above, material parts of Witness 101's account are inconsistent with the physical and forensic evidence, internally inconsistent from one part of his account to the next, and inconsistent with other credible witness accounts that are corroborated by physical evidence. It is also unclear whether Witness 101 had the ability to accurately perceive the shootings. Witness 101 likely crouched down next to a white Monte Carlo as Wilson chased Brown. The Monte Carlo was facing west with a view of the passenger side of the SUV. Brown ran in the opposite direction that the Monte Carlo was facing. Witness accounts vary as to whether Witness 101 was ducking for cover on the passenger side of the Monte Carlo with his back to the shooting, or whether he fled the scene prior to the final shots being fired. Both Witness 101's inconsistencies and his ability to perceive what happened, or lack thereof, make his account vulnerable to effective cross-examination and extensive impeachment. Accordingly, after a thorough review of all of the evidence, federal prosecutors determined material portions of Witness 101's account lack credibility and therefore determined that his account does not support a prosecution of Darren Wilson.

ii. **Witness 123**

Witness 123 is a 29-year-old black male who gave two statements. First, he was jointly interviewed by FBI agents and SLCPD detectives. Second, he testified before the county grand jury.

Witness 123 was in the front passenger seat of a white Monte Carlo that was traveling west on Canfield Drive behind Wilson before Wilson stopped his SUV. Witness 133, a black female, was driving the Monte Carlo. Witness 123 first observed Brown and his friend, Witness 101, walking in the street in the opposite direction of the SUV. It seemed to Witness 123 that Brown and Witness 101 failed to comply with a directive from Wilson because the SUV quickly swerved back, and stopped while Brown and Witness 101 were still standing on the yellow line in the middle of the street.

The SUV was then positioned such that Witness 123 and Witness 133 had a view of its passenger side. Therefore, although Witness 123 described a tussle involving Brown at the driver's window, he could not be more specific. During the tussle, Witness 101 looked startled and ran off. Witness 123 then heard a gunshot and told Witness 133 to back up. He heard a second gunshot just as Brown was running past the driver's window of the Monte Carlo. Witness 123 ducked after the second shot and, therefore, could not see if Brown was injured. Between four and six seconds later, he looked out the front windshield to see Wilson emerge from the SUV with his gun held low. At about the same time, Witness 101 approached the Monte Carlo's passenger side door, which Witness 123 had already opened to allow him more room to duck. Witness 101 asked if he could get into their car, but Witness 123 would not permit him to do so, instead instructing him to duck down. Witness 123 then turned his attention to Witness 133, who was shaking. While Witness 123 attempted to calm Witness 133, Witness 101 disappeared and they never saw him again.

Witness 123 explained to the FBI and the SLCPD that he turned around and watched through the back window as Brown turned around with hands half-way up, shoulder height, and crunched up as though he was about to go to the ground. Witness 123 did not know what prompted Brown to turn around. He then heard a volley of about five shots in addition to the two initial shots, and Brown fell forward to his death, palms face forward and arms tucked under him. Witness 123 told the county grand jury that he saw Brown turn around and hold his hands up. Wilson shot Brown three times and Brown fell to the ground dead. Contrary to the physical evidence, Witness 123 explained that Brown died where he turned around and did not move toward Wilson. After the final shots, Wilson appeared to be looking at his (Wilson's) arms.

Witness 133 quickly drove around the SUV and away from the scene after the shooting. Witness 123 and Witness 133 subsequently discussed what they had seen with each other while watching media reports.

Witness 123 has no criminal history. Witness 123's accounts to investigators and to the county grand jury were inconsistent with the physical and forensic evidence, making him vulnerable to effective cross-examination. His focus was split among the driver of the vehicle, Witness 101, and the shooting itself. For those reasons, prosecutors questioned his ability to accurately perceive the incident and could not rely upon his account to support prosecution of Darren Wilson.

iii. **Witness 133**

Witness 133 is a 33-year-old black female who gave three statements. SLCPD detectives first interviewed Witness 133 within hours of the shooting. She subsequently met with federal agents and prosecutors who questioned her more in-depth. She then testified before the county grand jury.

As previously noted, Witness 133 was driving a white Monte Carlo west on Canfield Drive when she was forced to stop behind Wilson's SUV. Witness 123 was seated in Witness 133's front passenger seat. Witness 133 initially saw Brown and Witness 101 walking down the center line of the street in the opposite direction in which she was traveling. Wilson stopped his SUV alongside Brown and Witness 101, and it appeared to Witness 133 that "something had to have been said between the two parties." However, Witness 133 could not hear anything. Once the SUV stopped, her vantage point was of its passenger side. She was able to see that there was some sort of "tussle" on the driver's side of the SUV between Wilson, who was seated in the SUV, and Brown, whose feet she could see moving underneath the SUV. The SUV was shaking. Witness 101, who was standing closer to the front of the SUV, was trying to see what was happening.

Witness 133 then heard a gunshot from within the SUV. Witness 133 stated that the "suspect who got shot, backed up, and seemed amazed." Both Brown and Witness 101 then ran eastbound past her vehicle down Canfield Drive. The gunshot "terrified" Witness 133, and when she saw Wilson get out of the SUV, she immediately ducked down for cover. It was then that Witness 101 appeared at her passenger side door, asking if he could get in the car, saying "Can you get me away from here? It's crazy." Witness 133 refused to allow Witness 101 into her car, instead telling him to duck. Witness 123, Witness 133, and Witness 101 all ducked for cover together. During her interview with federal authorities, Witness 133 added that she likely "blacked out" while all of this was happening.

Shortly thereafter, Witness 133 looked in her rearview mirror, and saw Brown's face, indicating to her that Brown had turned to face Wilson. She described hearing two or three shots and then Brown fell to the ground. At some point, Witness 101 disappeared, but having been focused on Brown, she did not know where he went or when he left. Wanting to leave quickly, Witness 133 drove on the grass and around the SUV to get out of the area.

During both her interview with SLCPD and her follow-up interview with federal agents and prosecutors, Witness 133 was repeatedly asked if there was anything else that she saw or anything she thought investigators would need to know. In both instances, Witness 133 denied knowing any more information, telling federal authorities that she had given "everything [she's] got." However, she expressed sorrow as the mother of a teenaged son.

Despite her repeated assurances that she saw nothing else, Witness 133 testified before the county grand jury that when she looked in the rearview mirror, Brown had his hands up before he fell to his death. When questioned by the county prosecutor about providing this new information, Witness 133 acknowledged that the transcripts from her prior statements were correct, and that she told SLCPD detectives, FBI agents and federal prosecutors everything she could think of that was important. Witness 133 never offered an explanation as to why she did not previously disclose that Brown's hands were up. Witness 133 also acknowledged that she has been watching the news and "hands up" had become the "mantra" of the protesters.

Witness 133 has no criminal history. Witness 133's repeated omission of a material detail that goes directly to whether Wilson used unreasonable force, coupled with the fact that she told federal authorities that she "blacked out" before later testifying that she saw Brown's hands up, would subject her to effective cross-examination if called as a prosecution witness. It calls into question whether she actually saw Brown's hands at all, had "blacked out," or had been distracted by Witness 101. Accordingly, federal prosecutors determined material portions of her account to be unreliable, and therefore it does not support a prosecution of Darren Wilson.

iv. **Witness 119**

Witness 119 is a 15-year-old black male. He initially told SLCPD detectives that he witnessed the shooting. However, he later recanted, telling federal agents and prosecutors that he lied to SLCPD detectives because he just wanted to be involved in the investigation. Witness 119 reiterated the same thing to county prosecutors and did not testify before the county grand jury.

Witness 119 initially spoke to SLCPD detectives within hours of the shooting, while standing on Canfield Drive. In part because of the chaos around him during the interview, and in larger part because he was lying, much of Witness 119's initial account did not make sense. Witness 119 seemed to claim that Wilson shot Brown in the side from out of the window of the

SUV, possibly while he was still driving. Wilson then chased after Brown, and ultimately shot him to death in the head while Brown had his hands in the air.

Federal agents and prosecutors sought to follow up with Witness 119 to clarify his account. Witness 119 readily admitted that he never saw the shooting, but was sitting near a flowerbed playing video games on his phone when he heard gunshots. Witness 119 could not see the SUV from his vantage point. He and his brother waited until the gunshots stopped before going to the scene because they did not want to get hit by a stray bullet. By the time they arrived on scene, Brown was dead. Witness 119 claimed that he told the police that he was a witness because he was traumatized and because he "wanted to be a part of it."

Because Witness 119 admitted that he gave a false account, federal prosecutors did not consider his account in the prosecutive decision.

v. **Witness 125**

Witness 125 is a 23-year-old black female. She initially told law enforcement that she witnessed the shooting, but later recanted, claiming that she wanted to be involved from the outset and therefore lied to investigators.

SLCPD detectives briefly interviewed Witness 125 during their initial canvass after the shooting. Witness 125 claimed that she was asleep for the first two gunshots. Her boyfriend, Witness 131, told her to get up and go to the window. Witness 125 then gave an internally inconsistent account, first saying that Brown's arms were by his waist, followed by his hands going up. When asked for clarification, she said the same thing in reverse, explaining that it all occurred while Brown was kneeling.

In an effort to reconcile this inconsistency and help inform the prosecutive decision, federal prosecutors sought to meet with Witness 125. Witness 125 refused to meet with federal prosecutors but did meet with FBI agents. She reiterated that she was asleep during the first few shots, but then went to her window where she witnessed Brown standing with his hands up in surrender. Although she could not see who was shooting Brown due to a tree blocking her line of sight, Witness 125 explained that she witnessed two volleys of shots, one which caused Brown to grab his torso with his left hand and a second volley causing his head to snap back before he fell to the ground. Witness 125 did not see Brown move from his position. Despite saying otherwise in her recorded statement to the SLCPD, she denied telling FBI agents that she originally told SLCPD detectives that Brown was kneeling prior to his death.

When Witness 125 appeared at the St. Louis County Prosecutor's Office to testify before the county grand jury, she was accompanied by an attorney. Prior to her testimony, Witness 125 told the county prosecutors that she lied to the FBI and to SLCPD detectives. Witness 125 was then given immunity from federal prosecution for making material false statements to federal agents so long as she testified truthfully in the grand jury. She testified that she did not, in fact, witness any part of the incident, but claimed she did so because she wanted to be "part of something." She claimed that a friend in the community told her to tell the SLCPD and the FBI what her boyfriend saw, but to claim it as her own.

Witness 125 has no criminal history. Because Witness 125 admitted that she gave false accounts, federal prosecutors did not consider her accounts in the prosecutive decision.

vi. **Witness 131**

Witness 131 is a 22-year-old black male. As previously mentioned, Witness 131 is the fiancé of Witness 125, who first told SLCPD detectives and then FBI agents that she saw Wilson shoot Brown while he had his hands in the air, and then admitted to county prosecutors that she lied to law enforcement and did not, in fact, see anything. Witness 131 gave two statements, first to FBI agents and then he testified before the county grand jury.

Witness 131 told the FBI that he was in his apartment when he heard three gunshots, prompting him to call Witness 125 to come look out their living room window. However, he changed his account when he testified before the county grand jury, claiming that he only called to his fiancée once the shooting had stopped.

Witness 131 stated that he initially did not see Wilson, but saw only Brown, who was taking a few steps forward. Witness 131 testified before the county grand jury that his view was somewhat obstructed, but he also saw Witness 101 run across the yard. Witness 131 then heard about five more shots, and watched as Brown grabbed his torso with his left hand, while holding his right hand in the air, in front him at a 45 degree angle. Witness 131 then heard another volley of shots and Brown's arms dropped. Brown fell to his knees and collapsed face down in the street. Witness 131 explained to the FBI that once Brown stopped moving forward, the shooting stopped. It was then that Witness 131 noticed a police officer approach Brown just as other officers arrived on scene.

Despite Witness 131 telling the FBI that Brown was shot only when he moved forward, he testified to the contrary in front of the county grand jury. There, he testified that Brown stood still as he was shot to death and denied that Brown moved forward at all. When county prosecutors confronted Witness 131 with his inconsistency, he denied that he said anything different to the FBI.

Witness 131 has no criminal history. Witness 131's accounts are inconsistent with each other, and his most recent version is inconsistent with the physical and forensic evidence. He also claimed that his fiancée was present for something she admitted she did not witness. Accordingly, based on a thorough review of all of the evidence, federal prosecutors determined his account not to be credible, and it therefore does not support a prosecution of Darren Wilson.

vii. **Witness 112**

Witness 112 is a 62-year-old black male who was with his brother, Witness 110, and sister-in-law, Witness 111, when he witnessed the shooting. As described above, they witnessed the shooting from the second floor balcony located opposite and off to the right of the minivan occupied by Witness 104, Witness 105, Witness 106, and Witness 107. Their view was of the passenger side of the SUV, followed by the right profile of Brown as he ran away from Wilson, and then the left profile of Brown as he turned around and moved toward Wilson.

Witness 112 gave three investigative statements, and he also spoke to the print media. He spoke first with SLCPD detectives. He then met with federal prosecutors and agents, and subsequently testified before the county grand jury.

Witness 112 agreed to meet with SLCPD detectives only because he spoke to his pastor, and realized that what he witnessed was "weighing on [him]." Witness 112 explained that Witness 101 could not have seen what he is claiming to have seen in his media interviews. According to Witness 112, he was sitting by his bedroom window when he saw Brown and Witness 101 walking in the center of the street. Witness 112 knew Brown from the neighborhood and always found him to be respectful.

Witness 112 saw Wilson's SUV pass Brown and Witness 101, and then back up. Witness 112 then went out to his balcony to get a better view. Once there, he saw a "tussling" at the SUV, and acknowledged that he did not know whether Wilson grabbed Brown or vice versa. However, Witness 112 was adamant that, contrary to what he kept hearing from people in his neighborhood, at least one of Brown's arms was inside the SUV. Wilson fired a shot from within the SUV, likely in an effort to get Brown off of him because Brown was so big. After that initial shot, Brown looked startled and took off running. Witness 101 took off running as well, and did not reappear until much later, once Brown's body was covered.

Witness 112 explained that it appeared that Brown stopped running because either the pain or shock hit him. Brown turned around, and looked down, as though checking himself for injury. In so doing, Witness 112 explained that Brown raised his arms partly, palms up, clarifying that he "didn't have his hands all the way up." Brown then moved his arms out at a 35 to 45 degree angle, as if to say, "What?" It was then that Wilson trained his gun on Brown, and as Brown moved forward, Wilson repeatedly yelled, "Stop!" When Brown failed to stop, Wilson fired shots. Brown's arms went limp at his sides, but he kept moving toward Wilson, though Witness 112 characterized it as "not in a menacing way." Witness 112 explained that at no time did Brown say a word. Instead, Witness 112 yelled out from his balcony for Brown to stop, but Brown kept slowly advancing, bent forward, and Wilson kept shooting.

When Witness 112 subsequently met with federal agents and prosecutors, he gave a similar account, except that he steadfastly claimed that when Brown turned around in the roadway, he held his arms up in surrender, at ninety degree angles with his palms facing out. When asked about his previous description, Witness 112 became agitated and angry, and refused to listen to a recording of his previous statement. He was unable to explain the difference in his accounts, and why his statement had changed. Witness 112 similarly described that Brown held his hands up in surrender when he testified before the county grand jury.

Subsequent to his meeting with federal authorities and his appearance before the county grand jury, Witness 112 gave an "anonymous" interview to the local print media. Although Witness 112 never identified himself, based on the account given that was almost verbatim to his initial SLCPD interview and the proximity in time to his county grand jury testimony, federal and county prosecutors and investigators recognized that it was Witness 112. In that media interview, Witness 112 reverted to his initial version that he told SLCPD detectives, explaining that Brown did not have his hands up in surrender, but rather partly raised his arms, palms up, checking for injury. This stood in stark contrast to what he told the FBI and federal prosecutors, and to his testimony in the county grand jury.

Witness 112 has a felony conviction for stealing from 18 years ago that likely would be inadmissible in federal court as impeachment evidence. Witness 112 made it clear in all of his statements that he believes that Wilson should not have shot and killed Brown, stating that it was "overkill," without offering more of an explanation. Witness 112's accounts are inconsistent as to whether Brown held his hands up in surrender, and his most recent account is that Brown's hands were not up in surrender. Because federal prosecutors cannot discern the truth among Witness 112's versions, and his most recent account does not inculpate Wilson, federal prosecutors cannot rely upon it to support a prosecution of Darren Wilson.

viii.   **Witness 135**

Witness 135 is a 20-year-old black female. She was walking on Canfield Drive at the time of the initial interaction between Brown and Wilson. She gave three statements. The FBI first interviewed Witness 135 during their canvass on August 16, 2014, and she subsequently met with federal prosecutors. She then testified before the county grand jury.

According to Witness 135, as she was standing on the south side of the street, she saw Wilson's SUV back up and bump up against Brown and his friend. Brown then "charged over" to the driver's side of the SUV and put his arms inside the driver's window. She was unable to see what transpired inside the vehicle because the width of Brown's back obstructed her view. She did, however, explain that Brown's arms were moving aggressively and his head, shoulders, and top half of his body were in the window.

Witness 135 stated that this interaction lasted about 15 seconds during which time she saw a gun fall to the ground and then heard a gunshot. She moved to a nearby tree where she initially waited, and then continued her walk home. Brown ran anywhere from five to 10 steps, and then turned around to face Wilson who had emerged from the SUV seconds after Brown took off running. Witness 135 explained that she was both walking away and scanning the street as this was happening, so she did not see the entire incident. She recalled that as Brown turned around, he put his hands up with his arms, "scrunched up," pulled tight against his body, palms out at about shoulder height. According to Witness 135, Brown was hunched forward, though he took a few steps backward, and was shot about five times before he fell to his death. According to Witness 135, there was only this one additional volley of shots after the initial shot, Brown never moved forward, and Wilson never shot Brown as he was running away.

Witness 135 readily acknowledged to federal prosecutors that she has poor vision, and was not wearing her contact lenses on the date of the shooting. She was able to see shapes and figures, but could not see details or facial expressions from where she stood once Brown ran from the SUV. Because the physical evidence proves that Brown moved forward before he fell to his death, federal prosecutors and agents asked Witness 135 if it was possible that Brown moved forward, but she did not see it. Witness 135 responded that it was possible, not only because of her vision problems but because she was not watching Brown the entire time. Instead, she was scanning the block, and was worried for her own safety due to the ringing of gunshots.

Witness 135 explained to federal prosecutors that Brown's friend ran off as soon as the first shot was fired and she never saw him again. However, she described a similarly built black male with dreadlocks who was later running around the Canfield apartments, saying something to the effect of, "The police shot my friend and his hands were up." Witness 135 explained that quickly became the narrative on the street, and to her frustration, people used it both as an excuse to riot and to create a "block party" atmosphere.

During her county grand jury testimony, Witness 135 characterized Wilson's actions as "murder," an opinion that would be inadmissible in federal court. When county prosecutors pressed her for an explanation, she stated that she sees it that way because Wilson should have used a taser, night stick, or similar weapon. Witness 135 also stated that when she saw the gun drop by the SUV, she assumed it belonged to Brown, acknowledging that it was not unreasonable for Wilson to think that Brown had a weapon. Witness 135 also testified about her own negative experience with the FPD, when an officer arrested her and "basically beat [her] up." That officer was not Darren Wilson, nor did she ever have prior interactions with Wilson.

Witness 135 has no criminal history. As detailed above, Witness 135's initial account was inconsistent with the forensic and physical evidence and inconsistent with other credible witness accounts. She admittedly was unsure of what she saw, both because she was distracted and because she has poor vision. Because of her admitted inconsistencies along with her questionable ability to have accurately perceived what happened, federal prosecutors determined material parts of this witness's account to lack reliability and therefore, her account does not support a prosecution of Darren Wilson

ix. **Witness 124**

Witness 124 is a 31-year-old black female. As previously noted, Witness 124 is the wife of Witness 115. In addition to testifying before the county grand jury, Witness 124 gave two interviews to law enforcement, first to SLCPD detectives and then to FBI agents during their canvass one week after the shooting.

In her initial interview to SLCPD detectives, Witness 124 explained that she was on the phone and eating when her husband, Witness 115, called to her, "Baby, Look out the window. They're shooting." She went to the window and saw Brown running from Wilson, who was walking and steadily shooting at Brown from behind. Brown then disappeared from her sight, making her think that Brown got away. However, Brown then reappeared and came back toward Wilson. Witness 124 then joined Witness 115 on the balcony with their three children. Once on the balcony, Witness 124 saw Wilson shoot Brown in the chest area, firing two shots, followed by three shots until Brown tipped over and fell to the pavement. She further told the SLCPD detective that Brown had nothing in his hands, and Wilson did not go near Brown's body. At no point did Witness 124 describe Brown's arm across his torso as her husband described. At no point did she describe Brown's hands up in surrender.

However, during her interview with the FBI, Witness 124 described that she first saw Wilson's SUV when Wilson tried to run over Brown and Witness 101. This directly contradicts her prior statement that Witness 115 called to her to look out the window after the first shots were fired. During her FBI interview, Witness 124 also added that she saw Brown turn around and put his hands up. This also directly contradicts her initial statement in which she claimed that Brown disappeared from sight and that she did not see him until he reappeared in her line of sight. Witness 124 also added that, contrary to virtually every other witness account, Wilson walked toward Brown and shot him to death.

Witness 124 has no criminal history. In an effort to reconcile the apparent inconsistencies in Witness 124's accounts and determine what she actually witnessed as opposed to what she may have heard from others, federal prosecutors sought to meet with her. However, Witness 124 failed to appear for a scheduled meeting and refused to reschedule at any time or place of her convenience. Therefore, federal prosecutors did not have the opportunity to assess her credibility and determine which parts of her account, if any, were accurate. Because the substance of her two investigative accounts stood in stark contrast to each other, without further explanation, federal prosecutors determined her accounts not to be credible and therefore did not consider them in its prosecutive decision.

x. **Witness 127**

Witness 127 is a 27-year-old black female who gave three investigative statements, including testifying before the county grand jury. SLCPD detectives initially interviewed Witness 127 within two hours of the shooting. She subsequently appeared in the media several times. Federal agents and prosecutors interviewed Witness 127, in the presence of her lawyer, because parts of her account were inconsistent with the physical evidence.

According to Witness 127, she was driving east on Canfield Drive, traveling in the opposite direction of Wilson's SUV. and heard tires screeching as she rounded a curve. When she pulled up to where the SUV was stopped, Witness 127 saw Brown "rassling" at the driver's window. Brown's head was bent at the window, with his palms on the outside of the door. Witness 127 said that it looked like Brown was either pushing off of the door or pulling away and that someone was pulling him into the car, in a "tug of war" manner. However, she did not see anyone or anything pulling Brown. At the same time this was happening, Witness 127 was looking at her mobile phone, trying to no avail to record what was transpiring "because it didn't look right." Witness 127 then heard a gunshot, but did not see blood or injury. She said that Brown broke free, indicating that it looked like Brown's right shirtsleeve was being pulled, though she could not see anything pulling it.

Upon hearing that gunshot, Witness 127 drove around the SUV and turned left into a nearby parking lot. She parked her car and got out. By that time, she saw Brown running and heard shots being fired. Witness 127 did not actually see Wilson exit the SUV, but she saw him chase after Brown. Witness 127 described volleys of gunshots without specificity. She explained that once she was out of her car, she began walking on the sidewalk as the shooting continued. She saw Brown's body make a jerking movement such that his hands started going up involuntarily. In one quick motion, Brown turned around with his hands up at right angles at his shoulders. Wilson then shot him, and Brown fell to his death where he stood. Witness 127 did not see injury to either of Brown's hands when his hands were up. Witness 127 was adamant that, contrary to DNA evidence with regard to the blood east of Brown's body, Brown never moved toward Wilson. She insisted that he fell to his death right where he turned around. She was equally adamant that Brown's hands remained outside the SUV during the initial interaction between Wilson and Brown, despite forensic and physical evidence to the contrary. When questioned by federal prosecutors and then by county prosecutors during her county grand jury testimony, she disallowed any possibility that perhaps her perception was compromised because she was using her phone, driving, and parking, among other reasons. Additionally, Witness 127 appeared in the media with her friend, Witness 118, allowing for the possibility that their accounts became conflated .

Witness 127 has no criminal history. Although Witness 127's statements are materially consistent with each other, significant portions are contrary to the forensic and physical evidence and inconsistent with credible witness accounts. Witness 127 was unable to give reasonable explanations as to why the physical evidence might be inconsistent with what she remembers, and therefore prosecutors were left to conclude that she inaccurately perceived material portions of the shootings either because of the stress of incidents or because she was distracted. Accordingly, after a thorough review of the evidence, federal prosecutors determined material portions of this witness's account not reliable and therefore cannot be used to support prosecution of Darren Wilson.

xi. **Witness 118**

Witness 118 is a 19-year-old black female who lives in the Canfield Green neighborhood and knew Brown through a mutual friend, Witness 120. Witness 118 also knew Witness 101, with whom she became friendly when she moved into the neighborhood. Prior to the shootings, Witness 118 and Witness 101 socialized almost weekly. Witness 118 denied speaking with Witness 101 since the shootings, contrary to what Witness 101 said during his testimony before the county grand jury. However, Witness 118 acknowledged speaking to Witness 120 about the shooting. As detailed later in this memorandum, Witness 120 was admittedly untruthful about what he claimed to have witnessed.

Witness 118 gave three investigative statements, and testified before the county grand jury. A SLCPD detective initially interviewed Witness 118 approximately two hours after the shooting. She subsequently appeared in the media several times. During those media interviews, Witness 118 added details that she did not report to local law enforcement, claiming in the news that she saw the "whole scenario play out." In an effort to evaluate the inconsistencies between her statements to law enforcement and her statements to the media as well as inconsistencies with physical evidence, federal agents and prosecutors interviewed Witness 118 in the presence of her lawyer.

During her initial SLCPD interview, Witness 118 stated that just before the shooting, she was in her apartment when she heard the screech of tires and thought someone might be hurt. She then heard three gunshots and went to look out her bedroom window. Witness 118 denied to the SLCPD detective that she witnessed any "tussle" at the side of the SUV. In fact, her view was of the passenger side of the SUV, which would have limited her ability to see a struggle at the driver's side even if she had looked out the window in time.

Witness 118 told the SLCPD detective that she then saw Wilson get out of the SUV and run in a hurry. She did not see anyone else at that time. She left her bedroom window to go to her patio door when she heard no less than four more shots. Those shots occurred about 30 seconds after the first three shots. Witness 118 thought someone was trying to shoot Wilson. She did not see Brown until she got to her patio door, when she peeked through the blinds to see him running. While looking through her glass door, she was distracted for about 10 to 30 seconds by Witness 101 ducking behind a black Monte Carlo and trying to hide. Witness 101 was creeping westward, toward the front of the Monte Carlo, with his back to Wilson and Brown as they ran east on Canfield Drive.

Witness 118 told the SLCPD detective that she then looked back toward Brown as he turned around, put his hands in the air, and got shot two times. Brown fell to the ground face down, with his arms at 90 degree angles on either side of his head, contrary to what the crime scene photos depict and the SLCME medicolegal investigator noted, *i.e.,* Brown's left hand was at his waistband and his right hand was down at his side.

At the conclusion of the interview with the SLCPD, Witness 118 assured the detective that what she reported was her best recollection of the incident and that she was not leaving anything out. Nonetheless, Witness 118's accounts to the media and to federal prosecutors and agents were different from her initial statement to the SLCPD, even though her grand jury testimony was ultimately more consistent with her initial SLCPD account.

Witness 118 claimed to the media that she "saw" screeching tires as the SUV swerved at Brown and Witness 101. She further claimed that she watched Brown as he was reaching, pulling, and "hassling" through the window of the SUV, in what appeared to be "arm wrestling." Witness 118 told the media that Wilson was pulling Brown into the SUV while Brown was trying to flee. She claimed to have seen the first gunshots hit Brown as he pulled away and fled. She also claimed that she saw a bullet strike a nearby building, but acknowledged that she inferred this because she saw SLCPD detectives attempting to remove one from a building wall.

Witness 118 added to her media narrative that Wilson shot Brown in the back from three feet away and that Brown never moved back towards Wilson. Physical evidence is inconsistent with both of those added details. Also, contrary to her initial account, Witness 118 told federal agents and prosecutors that Brown's arms were at his sides and his hands were around his hips when he came to rest on the ground.

When federal prosecutors and agents challenged the inconsistencies in her accounts, Witness 118 conceded that she likely assumed facts that she did not witness herself based on talking with other residents in the Canfield Green complex and watching the news, but was not specific about which facts. Witness 118 also added that she did not have a lawyer when she was first interviewed by the SLCPD, though there was nothing to indicate that interview was custodial or coercive and Witness 118 expressed no apprehension or hesitation when speaking with the SLCPD.

Witness 118 has no criminal history. Witness 118's accounts are riddled with internal inconsistencies, inconsistencies with the physical and forensic evidence, and inconsistencies with credible witness accounts. Her attention was admittedly diverted away from the shooting when she watched Witness 101 ducking for cover and she acknowledged that her account was also based on assumption and media coverage. Accordingly, after a thorough review of the evidence, federal prosecutors determined the various versions of this witness's account to lack credibility and therefore it does not support a prosecution of Darren Wilson.

xii. **Witness 122**

Witness 122 is a 46-year-old white male. He was laying drain pipe on Canfield Drive with Witness 130 on the morning of the shooting. Witness 122 gave six statements, including testimony before the county grand jury. SLCPD detectives and an FBI agent twice jointly interviewed him, and SLCPD detectives once independently interviewed him. Witness 122 and Witness 130 authored one-page written statements on advice of a former boss. Witness 122 and Witness 130 claimed that they did not discuss what they witnessed, though Witness 130 admitted that they read each other's statements after they were written. Witness 122 gave a media interview on the condition of anonymity. As noted throughout this memorandum, federal prosecutors interviewed many potential witnesses in an effort to assess credibility and reconcile internal inconsistencies and inconsistencies with physical evidence, as is necessary to make a fair prosecutive decision. Witness 122 agreed to meet with federal prosecutors only after assurances that he would not be held against his will at the FBI office, claiming that he had heard of instances where individuals go to the FBI office and do not emerge for days.

According to Witness 122, Witness 122 and Witness 130 (collectively, "the contractors") twice encountered Brown during the morning of the shootings, first when Brown was alone and then when Brown was with Witness 101. Witness 122 and Brown did most of the talking, and the topics included God and smoking marijuana. About 20 minutes after their last conversation with Brown, the contractors heard a loud bang. Witness 122 saw Brown running, staggering, or falling forward. Contrary to the autopsy results, Witness 122 described Brown being shot in the back and "knew he had gotten hit." In fact, both contractors claimed to have witnessed bullets go through Brown and exit his back, as evidenced by his shirt "popping back" and "stuff coming through." However, in his interview with federal prosecutors, Witness 122 explained that he thought that Brown was shot in the back and stumbled until he saw media reports about the autopsy commissioned by Brown's family. After learning about that autopsy, he realized that Brown was not shot in the back and admittedly changed his account.

Witness 122 also claimed that Brown put his right hand to the ground to regain his balance when he was hit and as he turned around. According to both contractors, Brown then turned around with his hands up and repeatedly screamed "Okay!" as many as eight times, an exclamation heard by no other witness. When Witness 122 demonstrated the position of

Brown's hands for federal prosecutors and agents, he wavered from a position of surrender to one indicative of a person trying to maintain balance.

Contrary to the autopsy results establishing that the shot to the top of Brown's head would have incapacitated Brown almost immediately, both contractors insisted that Brown continued to move toward Wilson as far as 20, 25, or even 30 feet after the final shots. Witness 122 described Brown as walking "dead on his feet, and then he just fell forward." Later, both contractors admitted that they did not actually see Brown fall to the ground, because their view was obstructed by the corner of a building.

Witness 122 insisted that there were three officers present during the shootings, demonstrating the inaccuracy of his perception. Witness 122 described three uniformed police officers engaged with Brown in a "triangle formation" at the time of the shootings. Witness 122 described a heavyset, older officer, and two "skinny, little people," one of whom was possibly a female and the other with dark hair and a moustache, who was a head shorter than the heavyset officer. Witness 122 described the shooter as the heavyset officer. Witness 122 explained that the heavset officer shot until he ran out of bullets, and then the shorter officer with the moustache trained his gun on Brown, but did not shoot. These statements cannot be reconciled with the fact that Wilson was the only officer present when Brown was shot and that Wilson has a slim build.

Witness 122 also explained that he did not see Witness 101 at all during the shooting itself, and did not understand how Witness 101 could claim to see everything if he was hiding behind a car. Witness 122 also said that contrary to what was reported in the media, Brown did not say, "Don't shoot."

The contractors, apparently unwittingly, were captured on a widely circulated video taken several minutes after the shooting while responding officers were securing the scene with crime scene tape. That video depicts another individual yelling, "He wasn't no threat at all," as Witness 122 put his hands up and stated, "He had his fucking hands in the air." As detailed below, two other witnesses, Witness 128 and Witness 137, each took credit for making the statement, "He wasn't no threat at all."[24] Both of those witnesses have since acknowledged to federal agents and prosecutors that they did not, in fact, know whether Brown was a threat.

According to the Brown family, Witness 122 called them after the shooting and told them that he had seen Wilson shoot Brown execution-style as Brown was on his knees holding his hands in the air. However, Witness 122 denied making any statements about the nature of the shooting to the Brown family. As mentioned, despite his earlier statements, Witness 122 recanted the claim that he actually saw Brown fall dead to the ground.

Witness 122 has no criminal history. As detailed above, material portions of Witness 122's accounts are irreconcilable with the physical and forensic evidence. These accounts are also inconsistent with each other and inconsistent with credible witness accounts. Accordingly, after a thorough review of all of the evidence, federal prosecutors determined this witness's accounts not to be credible and therefore do not support a prosecution of Darren Wilson.

---

[24] The person who recorded this video claimed that yet another person, "Chris," made that statement.

xiii. **Witness 130**

Witness 130 is a 26–year-old white male. As previously noted, he was laying drain pipe on Canfield Drive with Witness 122, on the morning of the shooting. Witness 130 gave five statements, including testimony before the county grand jury. SLCPD detectives and an FBI agent twice jointly interviewed him, and SLCPD detectives once independently interviewed him. Like Witness 122, Witness 130 authored a one-page written statement on advice of a former boss. Witness 122 and Witness 130 claimed that they did not discuss what they witnessed, though Witness 130 admitted that they read each other's statements after they were written. Like Witness 122, Witness 130 gave a media interview on the condition of anonymity.

As noted, Witness 122 and Witness 130 twice encountered Brown during the morning of the shootings, first when Brown was alone and then when Brown was with Witness 101. Witness 122 and Brown did most of the talking, and Witness 130 admitted that at times, Brown seemed paranoid and aggressive, clenching his fists and causing Witness 130 some concern. Witness 130 thought Brown "was not in his right mind," based upon how paranoid he seemed.

About 20 minutes after their last conversation with Brown, Witness 130 heard a loud bang. Witness 130 stepped around the corner of an apartment building that was obstructing his view, and saw Brown "fast walk[ing]" east on Canfield Drive. According to both contractors, Brown then turned around with his hands up and repeatedly screamed "Okay!" as many as eight times, an exclamation heard by no other witness According to Witness 130, after Brown turned around, he continued to stumble or otherwise approach Wilson, although he did not know whether Brown was speeding up to come after Wilson, or whether his momentum was carrying him forward. Wilson then fired at least seven shots, but as Witness 130 told the grand jury, Wilson only fired when Brown moved forward. Witness 130 described Wilson "unloading his clip" into Brown, although Witness 130 acknowledged that Brown put his arms down after the third shot.

Witness 130 explained that Wilson backed up as Brown approached him. Contrary to the autopsy results establishing that the shot to the top of Brown's head would have incapacitated Brown almost immediately, like Witness 122, Witness 130 insisted that Brown continued to move toward Wilson as far as 20, 25, or even 30 feet after the final shots. Contrary to his initial account, Witness 130 admitted that he did not actually see Brown fall to the ground because his view was obstructed by the corner of a building.

Witness 130 has no criminal history. Federal prosecutors attempted to meet with Witness 130 to evaluate inconsistencies in his various statements. Witness 130 refused to meet with federal prosecutors, making reliance on his account problematic because his statements are inconsistent with each other, inconsistent with the physical and forensic evidence, and inconsistent with credible witness accounts. Therefore, federal prosecutors could not rely on Witness 130's account to support a prosecution of Darren Wilson.

xiv. **Witness 142**

Witness 142 is a 48-year-old black male. Witness 142 briefly spoke to SLCPD detectives within hours of the shooting incident and denied that he witnessed the shooting. However, the

SLCPD and the FBI then followed up with Witness 142 after SLCPD detectives learned that Witness 142 called in to an Atlanta-based podcast on August 11, 2014, where he described the shootings. Witness 142 then testified before the county grand jury.

During the podcast, Witness 142 explained that he was sitting on his front patio when he heard the first gunshot. He then moved closer to get a better look at what he termed a "scuffle," and saw "the brother (referring to Brown) leaning over into the window." Witness 142 further described Brown's "upper body in the windshield." The podcast announcer then asked if what "the officer is saying is true," relative to what happened at the SUV. Witness 142 responded, "yes." Witness 142 explained that Brown then took off running and Wilson chased after him. Witness 142 thought that Wilson shot at Brown while Brown was running away. Brown then turned around and came back toward Wilson. Wilson "unloaded on him" and Brown fell to the ground.

The podcast announcer then asked if Brown's hands were up. Witness 142 responded, "Well, I don't know. I didn't see that." He went on to explain that "the crowd" was saying that Brown's hands were up, and that he was ducking to avoid getting hit by gunfire. The announcer later asked, "If you had to say from your opinion, was it justified?" Witness 142 paused and then said, "yes," referencing the scuffle in the SUV. However, he then stated that Wilson should not have shot at Brown while Brown was "fleeing the scene," an opinion that would be inadmissible in federal court and a misstatement of applicable federal law.

SLCPD detectives recognized Witness 142's voice on the podcast from their initial canvass of Canfield Drive, when Witness 142 denied seeing anything. Therefore, an SLCPD detective and an FBI agent interviewed Witness 142 again in an effort to determine what he actually saw. However, during that interview, Witness 142 again changed his account from what he stated on the podcast. Witness 142 told the SLCPD detective and the FBI agent that he was inside his apartment and heard one gunshot. He looked out his patio sliding glass door and saw the driver's side of a police SUV, where Brown was "tussling" with Wilson, who was inside the SUV. Witness 142 stated that Wilson was tugging on Brown's shirt collar. Even though Brown's back was to him, Witness 142 saw Brown's hands against the SUV and Wilson's hands grabbing Brown's shirt. He denied seeing any part of Brown's body inside the SUV. Brown then pushed away from the SUV and "sprinted" east on Canfield Drive. Wilson, with his gun on his hip, immediately got out of the SUV and chased Brown. After that, Witness 142 does not know what happened, claiming that a concrete barrier obstructed his view.

Witness 142 admitted that on the podcast, he stated that Brown's head was inside the SUV, but claimed that he lied, though he could offer no explanation for doing so. He recalled saying that Wilson shot Brown as Brown was running away, though he admitted to law enforcement that he did not see that happen. Witness 142 clarified that he thought Wilson was shooting at Brown because everything happened in a matter of seconds. He also acknowledged that he told the podcast announcer that he saw Brown stop, turn around, and come back at Wilson. However, he told the SLCPD detective and the FBI agent that he only assumed that Brown did those things, based on Brown's body facing west in the street. Witness 142 told law enforcement that he stayed outside in the street for hours after the shooting, hearing people say that Brown had his hands up. However, he did not see Brown with his hands up. Witness 142 stood by his initial statement that the shooting was justified, though he stated that he did not actually see what happened. He further told law enforcement that he originally lied to SLCPD detectives on the day of the shooting, when he claimed to not have seen anything. Witness 142 explained that he was afraid and did not want to get involved.

Witness 142 has no criminal history. Witness 142 changed his account and could offer no explanation as to why he did so, and his most recent account is inconsistent with credible witness accounts and inconsistent with forensic and physical evidence. Accordingly, federal prosecutors determined that they could not credit either one of his accounts. Regardless, his accounts do not inculpate Darren Wilson and therefore do not support a prosecution.

xv.   **Witness 138**

Witness 138 is a 22-year-old black male. The SLCPD first interviewed Witness 138 about five hours after the shooting. The interview was very brief and federal prosecutors and agents sought to interview him to obtain more detailed information. Witness 138 repeatedly ignored attempts by federal authorities to meet with him when he lived in St. Louis. He then moved out of state. Again, Witness 138 failed to respond to messages left by county and federal authorities, and refused to appear before the county grand jury. Finally, an FBI agent and federal prosecutor tracked down Witness 138 outside of his mother's house in Kentucky. Witness 138's account to federal authorites stood in stark contrast to what he initially told the SLCPD.

Witness 138 told SLCPD that on the day of the shooting, he was watching television in his apartment when he heard one gunshot, causing him to run outside. Brown had kicked off his flip flops and started running away from Wilson, who had emerged from his SUV with his gun drawn. Wilson ran east after Brown, past Witness 101 who was by a white Monte Carlo. Wilson shot Brown as he was running away. Brown then turned around, "threw his hands up," and said something. Initially, Witness 138 stated that he could not hear what Brown said. Then he explained that Brown said something with the word "shoot" in it. By the end of the interview, Witness 138 stated that Brown said, "Please don't shoot." Brown then fell to his knees, and Wilson shot him again. Other police officers arrived on the scene, and Wilson got into a different police vehicle than the one in which he arrived, and left the scene.

Witness 138 told federal authorities that Brown and Witness 101 came to his house the morning of the shooting, prior to their walk to Ferguson Market. They made plans to smoke marijuana later in the day and Brown and Witness 101 told Witness 138 that they were going to get cigarillos and would return. Thereafter, Witness 120 arrived at Witness 138's house. While Witness 138 and Witness 120 were talking in the doorway, Witness 138 heard two gunshots. He ran toward the gunshots, while Witness 120 ran in a different direction. Witness 138 saw Wilson "walk quickly" toward Brown. Unlike what he told the SLCPD detective, Witness 138 said that while going after Brown, Wilson was yelling "stop" or "freeze." Also contrary to his initial account, Witness 138 said that he did not hear Brown say anything. He saw Brown stop and put his hands up, shoulder height at 90 degree angles. Because he heard gunfire, Witness 138 ducked for cover, face-first in the dirt where two white contractors were working. Witness 138 remained in that position until the incident was over, and he looked up and saw Brown dead on the ground.

Witness 138 told federal authorities that Brown fell to the ground in the exact place where he first turned around and did not move forward toward Wilson. Because this is inconsistent with the physical evidence and other credible accounts, federal authorities asked Witness 138 if it was possible that Brown moved toward Wilson. Witness 138 explained that Brown could have moved forward, could have put his arms down, and in fact, he did not know what Brown did for the majority of the shooting because he was face-first in the dirt. He did not look up until Brown was already dead. Witness 138 described the position of Brown's body as having his hands at right angles next to his head, contrary to photographic evidence and the observations of the SLCME medicolegal investigator.

After Brown was killed, Witness 101 ran over to Witness 138 in shock. Witness 101 left the scene to change his clothes, and then returned. According to Witness 138, at the insistence of Witness 101's uncle and pastor, Witness 101 gave an interview to the media. Witness 138 explained that he was "stupid" to stand next to Witness 101 as he appeared on camera.

In response to federal authorities questioning about Wilson's description of Brown as "Hulk Hogan," Witness 138 said that Brown was more like the World Wrestling Federation wrestler "Big Show" in stature, but not in personality. Brown was intimidating because of his size, and Witness 138 understood how Wilson could generally perceive him as a threat. Witness 138 explained that he was friendly with Brown, and although it would surprise him if Brown attacked a police officer, it also surprised him to see the surveillance video of Brown shoving a store clerk, as it was uncharacteristic of him. In the days leading up to his death, Brown was acting out of character, speaking about his desire to get away from the struggles of life.

Witness 138 has no criminal history. There are significant inconsistencies between his two accounts, with the physical and forensic evidence, and with credible witness accounts. Accordingly, after a thorough review of the evidence, federal prosecutors determined this witness's first account to lack credibility. His second account, regardless of credibility, does not inculpate Wilson. Therefore, these accounts do not support a prosecution of Darren Wilson.

xvi. **Witness 132**

Witness 132 is a 25-year-old black male. He spoke with FBI agents on three occasions. First, Witness 132 met with FBI agents during their canvass on August 16, 2014. At that time, Witness 132 stated that he did not see the shooting or hear the gunshots. However, he stated that his wife may have seen some of the incident. Ten days later, two other FBI agents followed up with his wife. She indicated that she did not see anything, but Witness 132, contrary to what he stated before, claimed to have witnessed the shooting of Brown. Finally, Witness 132 spoke again to the FBI, claiming her memory of the shooting was "blurry."

During her second encounter with the FBI, contrary to all accounts that Wilson was driving westbound, Witness 132 said that he, Witness 132, was driving eastbound behind two FPD marked SUVs. Each SUV had two police officers, all of whom were white. According to Witness 132, the first SUV stopped in the middle of the street, cutting off Brown and running over his feet. Brown then "punched into the police car" because he was angry. In return, the police officer, to whom Witness 132 referred as "Ears," reached down and shot Brown. Witness

132 explained that Brown tried to run, but again, the officer shot Brown right where he stood, about five feet from the SUV. Brown half-turned, fell to his knees, and put his hands up. The officer shot Brown eight or nine more times. This all occurred on the passenger side of the vehicle.

After that interview with the FBI, Witness 132 actively and successfully evaded service of a county grand jury subpoena. Federal and county prosecutors independently and repeatedly tried to contact Witness 132 to no avail in an effort to reconcile the inconsistencies in his statements. However, Witness 132 ignored phone calls, hung up on the prosecutors, and pretended he was not at home. Witness 132 moved out of state and the FBI tracked him down in Georgia. Witness 132 refused to meet with federal prosecutors and told the FBI that the events of August 9, 2014 were "blurry," he could not remember what happened, and he was starting a new chapter in his life.

Witness 132 has no criminal history. Witness 132's second statement is starkly inconsistent with what he initially told law enforcement, is inconsistent with forensic and physical evidence, and is inconsistent with credible witness accounts. Federal prosecutors determined his account to inherently lack credibility, and did not consider it when making a prosecutive decision.

xvii. **Witness 121**

Witness 121 is a 36-year-old black female who twice spoke to federal authorities, and then testified before the county grand jury.

FBI agents initially interviewed Witness 121 in the presence of three other people during the FBI canvass on August 16, 2014. Her account was confusing and hard to follow, made more confusing by the three other individuals who interjected their thoughts into her account. Nonetheless, Witness 121 initially told the FBI that she saw Brown and Witness 101 walking in the street and she also saw an SUV with two police officers. The police officer on the driver's side of the SUV reached out from within the vehicle and grabbed Brown by the collar. She assumed that the officer had his hand on his gun when he grabbed Brown. She heard a gunshot which struck Brown in the upper chest, leaving a red spot on Brown's shirt. Witness 121 explained that the officer then immediately fired a second shot. Witness 121 seemed to suggest that the second shot happened while Brown was still by the SUV, prompting him to run; at another point during the same interview, Witness 121 suggested that the second shot occurred as Brown was running. She did not know whether that second shot struck Brown. She also explained that the second police officer emerged from the vehicle, though Witness 121 could not provide a description of him, nor be specific about when he emerged. Witness 121 explained that after Brown took off running, Brown put his hands up, walked toward Wilson, and then Wilson shot him. She further stated that Wilson walked over to Brown and "emptied" his gun into Brown, and that Brown "finally fell" after the last shot.

In contrast, however, during her follow up interview with federal prosecutors, Witness 121 explained that based on her vantage point, she did not see the initial interaction between Wilson and Brown. She explained that she had been standing by a dumpster, smoking a cigarette and talking on her phone when a gunshot drew her attention to the SUV. Once she heard the first shot, she became terrified and got ready to run, but instead watched Brown run from the SUV. Witness 121 made no mention of the second shot during her second interview. Likewise, Witness 121 denied that the second officer got out of the vehicle.

As before, Witness 121 explained that after Brown took off running, he put his hands up, walked toward Wilson, and then Wilson shot Brown. However, unlike in her first interview, Witness 121 denied that Wilson walked over to Brown and "emptied his gun" into him. Although she admitted making that prior statement, Witness 121 could offer no explanation for saying something that was inconsistent with the physical evidence and the accounts of almost all other witnesses. Instead, she described a chaotic scene and broke down in tears, acknowledging that she did not know what led up to the shooting. Witness 121 tearfully stated that she "didn't see that young man do anything wrong," empathizing with Brown's mother because her own mother lost a child.

Witness 121 confirmed during her interview with federal authorities that Wilson did not fire any shots while Brown was running way. According to Witness 121, the only shots fired were the first one and the volley of shots as Brown was walking toward the officer with his hands up in surrender. Contrary to how Brown's body was found and photographed when he fell to his death, Witness 121 was certain that Brown's body landed in the same position that his hands were in when he was standing, at right angles adjacent to his head.

Contrary to every other witness account and mobile phone video taken in the immediate aftermath of the shooting, Witness 121 explained that Wilson then checked Brown's pulse while his body lay on the ground. When federal prosecutors pressed her on this, Witness 121 acknowledged that perhaps she was mistaken. She stated that she was unsure which police officer checked his pulse and it likely happened after the police tape went up.

When asked about Witness 101's presence, Witness 121 explained that she had been looking back and forth between Brown and Witness 101 during the shooting. However, Witness 101's whereabouts were unclear throughout both of her accounts. During her first interview, Witness 121 stated that Witness 101 took off running when the initial shots were fired. During the second interview, she first stated that Witness 101 stood by the SUV and vomited on the street. When federal prosecutors asked if crime scene investigators would find vomit on the street to corroborate her claim, Witness 121 admitted that she did not see, but rather heard from others, that Witness 101 vomited on the street. Federal prosecutors and agents repeatedly urged Witness 121 to describe what she herself witnessed. It was then that she stated that Witness 101 had been crouched down, below car level, before he ran from the scene.

When Witness 121 appeared before the county grand jury, she again testified inconsistently. She testified that while she witnessed the shooting, she was standing next to Witness 126. As detailed below, Witness 126's account was internally inconsistent and inconsistent with physical evidence. She also claimed that Witness 137 tossed a cigarette down to her from a balcony above. Witness 137, as detailed below, admitted to being untruthful when he was first interviewed by the FBI, giving an account inconsistent with the physical evidence.

Reverting back to her initial account, Witness 121 testified before the county grand jury that even though her view was of the passenger side of the SUV, contrary to the physical evidence and other credible witnesses, Brown's hands were never inside the SUV. She also added that she heard Witness 101 tell Wilson that he and Brown "weren't that far" from where they were going.

Further, even though she admitted to federal prosecutors that she never heard Brown say anything, Witness 121 told the county grand jury that Brown screamed, "I give up!" as Wilson faced him in the roadway, gun drawn. However, she claimed that she was too far away to hear Wilson say anything.

Witness 121 has no criminal history. Witness 121 admittedly made false statements during her initial interview, her accounts are inconsistent with each other, inconsistent with the physical and forensic evidence, inconsistent with credible accounts, and she demonstrated bias in favor of Brown's family. Accordingly, after a thorough review of all of the evidence, federal prosecutors determined this witness's accounts to lack credibility and therefore do not support a prosecution of Darren Wilson.

xviii. **Witness 126**

Witness 126 is a 53-year-old black female. She is the godmother of Witness 137. Witness 126 gave two statements, first to the FBI and then to the county grand jury. During the course of her interview with the FBI, Witness 126 stated that her godson had been shot by police.

According to Witness 126, she suffers from memory loss and is under psychiatric care. Her account to the FBI was brief and is inconsistent with the autopsy results. She claimed that she was outside of her apartment during the shooting, never mentioning Witness 121 who claimed to be with Witness 126 at the time. Witness 126 saw Brown on his knees with his hands up, as Wilson was coming toward him and shooting at him. Brown then fell face down to the ground. Wilson went over to him, and similar to what her godson, Witness 137, said, "finished him off." When the FBI told Witness 126 that her account was contrary to the evidence, she became belligerent, grabbed the recording device, shut it off, and would not return it to the agents.

When the agents retrieved it, and turned the recording device back on, Witness 126 admitted that she initially lied. She stated that she never saw Wilson inflict gunshot wounds on Brown. Rather, she saw him running from behind, and then fall to his knees with his hands in the air. She then saw Wilson walking toward Brown, followed by a "click click" sound. Wilson had bruising and redness on the right side of his face. Someone then tapped her on the shoulder and she turned away. She heard nine gunshots in total, and by the time she turned back around, Brown was dead on the ground.

Witness 126 stated that she had spoken with Brown before. They discussed college and helping senior citizens. Brown told her that "everything he used to do, he wouldn't do it anymore."

Witness 126 telephoned the FBI the day after her interview to schedule an interview because she did not remember meeting with the agents and giving her account.

When Witness 126 testified before the county grand jury, she claimed to suffer from memory loss, but then recounted everything she had eaten for breakfast and every pill she had taken on the morning of August 9, 2014. Then she testified that she heard several shots, came out onto the parking lot, and saw Brown on his knees as Wilson fired shots into his head. She denied being untruthful to the FBI, and denied that she admitted to being untruthful to the FBI.

After Witness 126 testified before the county grand jury, she told the state prosecutor that she recorded the shooting on her mobile phone. However, she had since dropped the phone in the toilet. When the state prosecutor told her that forensic experts may still be able to recover the data, Witness 126 stated that she got mad and threw the phone in the junk yard.

Witness 126 has several felony arrests and a misdemeanor conviction that likely would be inadmissible in federal court as impeachment evidence. However, Witness 126 was admittedly untruthful to the FBI, suffers from memory loss, and provided internally inconsistent accounts that are also inconsistent with the physical and forensic evidence and credible witness accounts. Her account would be subject to extensive cross examination. Accordingly, federal prosecutors determined this witness's account to lack credibility and therefore it does not support a prosecution of Darren Wilson.

xix. **Witness 137**

Witness 137 is 40-year-old black male. After the shooting, Witness 137 had learned that Brown was his nephew's friend. He is the godson of Witness 126. He gave two law enforcement statements and testified before the county grand jury. Witness 137 first met with FBI agents on August 16, 2014, during their neighborhood canvass. Witness 137 also gave an interview to the media which was widely circulated throughout various media outlets. The account to the media and to the FBI was both internally inconsistent and inconsistent with the physical evidence. Therefore, federal agents and prosecutors subsequently met with Witness 137 in an attempt to assess inconsistencies and clarify his statement.

In his initial account during the neighborhood canvass, Witness 137 stated that he was on his porch using his mobile phone when he heard a gunshot. He looked out from his porch and saw Brown running away from a police officer who was chasing him. The police officer shot Brown in the back. "Realiz[ing] he was shot," Brown turned around with his hands up in surrender. Brown walked toward the officer and as he did so, the officer "closed in on him" until they were less than an arm's length apart. The officer fired "every round" into Brown, killing him "execution" style. Witness 137 explained that the officer shot Brown in the lower abdomen, chest, and then the "head shot." Witness 137 stated that after Brown fell forward, "the officer stood over him and finished him off." Witness 137 stated that the officer shot Brown in the head both when he was still standing and then when he was on the ground. Although Witness 137 stated that Brown fell to his knees for the final shots, and the last words Brown said were "Don't shoot," he also stated that Brown was lying on the ground when the final bullets were fired. Witness 137 referred to how clear the "visual" of events was to him.

Throughout the interview, Witness 137 also referred to events that preceded the initial gunshots even though he admitted that he did not see those events. He also discussed the interaction at the SUV, the location of recovered bullets, and the type of clip in the officer's gun.

During their follow-up interview with Witness 137, federal prosecutors and agents asked Witness 137 to describe only what he saw. Witness 137 once again stated that the sound of a gunshot drew his attention. When he moved further onto his porch, he said that he heard another shot, and saw Brown turn around with his hands up. Referencing the arm graze wound that was widely reported in the news after the privately-commissioned autopsy, Witness 137 stated that he believed that wound caused Brown to turn around. He then saw the officer backing up while firing shots as Brown walked at a "steady pace" of about ten steps in total toward him. According to Witness 137, there was no pause in the succession of shots, and Brown kept walking, even after he was shot in the torso. Witness 137 stated, "that's all I seen," explaining that he did not see Brown fall to the ground because that occurred in a blind spot. However, he was able to see the officer walk away, call for back up, and appear to be discombobulated. It was then that Witness 137 walked over to the scene where Brown's body lay in the street.

Contrary to his previous statement, Witness 137 denied that the officer shot Brown from less than an arm's length away, denied that he saw the officer shoot Brown execution-style; denied that the officer shot Brown when he was on the ground; denied that the officer "finished him off;" and denied that Brown's last words while on his knees were "Don't shoot." Witness 137 explained that he initially told the FBI that the officer stood over Brown and shot him execution-style while on his knees because he "assumed" that to be true. Witness 137 based his assumptions on the sound of the bullets and "common sense" from living in the community, despite claiming to have a "clear visual" of events.

Witness 137 also identified his voice on the aforementioned video taken in the aftermath of the shooting depicting the two contractors. As mentioned, Witness 137 was one of two people who claimed to be off camera shouting, "He wasn't no threat at all," because he did not perceive Brown to be a threat. However, Witness 137 acknowledged that contrary to what he originally told the FBI, the only part he saw was Brown moving back toward the officer. He did not witness what transpired at the SUV, did not witness Brown run from the SUV, and he did not witness Brown fall to his death. Therefore, Witness 137 agreed that he did not know whether Brown was a physical threat before or after the portion that Witness 137 claimed to see.

Witness 137 has previously been convicted of second-degree murder and armed criminal action which likely would be admissible in federal court as impeachment evidence. Additionally, Witness 137 was untruthful to the FBI during his initial interview, and untruthful in his media accounts. Although he later recanted most of what he claimed to have seen, he was unable to offer a credible explanation as to why he was not truthful at the outset, leaving federal prosecutors to question what, if anything, he actually did witness. His accounts are inconsistent with each other, inconsistent with the physical and forensic evidence, and inconsistent withcredible witness accounts. Accordingly, after a thorough review of the evidence, federal prosecutors determined this witness's accounts not to be credible and therefore do not support a prosecution of Darren Wilson.

xx.   **Witness 128**

Witness 128 is a 23-year-old black male who has made three different statements to law enforcement and testified before the county grand jury. He initially had a telephone interview with an investigator from the St. Louis County Prosecutor's Office and then an additional interview with that same investigator and the FBI. Both interviews were materially inconsistent with the physical evidence. Federal agents and prosecutors interviewed Witness 128 again in an effort to evaluate some of the inconsistencies.

According to Witness 128's initial accounts, he was driving east on Canfield Drive when he witnessed the shooting. It is unclear what Witness 128 initially saw because in one interview, he stated that he saw the police vehicle quickly back up. In another interview, he stated that by the time he pulled up, Wilson had already stopped his vehicle. Witness 128 stated that he then saw Brown struggling to get away from Wilson, who was choking Brown with both hands, while Witness 101 stood behind Brown. Witness 128 then heard a gunshot and saw the impact of the bullet, initially giving little detail but subsequently adding that Wilson held the gun out the window with his right hand while holding Brown with his left hand, and firing the gun into Brown's left chest.

Brown broke free and ran about 15 feet while Witness 101 ducked down between the police vehicle and the car right behind it. Witness 128 explained that while Wilson was still seated in the vehicle with the door closed, Wilson "let more shots go." Brown appeared to get hit by four rounds in the middle of his back. Brown "slowed up" and turned around, although Witness 128 later stated that Brown continued running another 20 or 25 feet before he turned around.

Wilson then emerged from the SUV about five seconds after he fired four or five rounds, and "patiently" walked toward Brown in "lazy pursuit." Brown "threw his hands up, clean in the air." Initially, Witness 128 stated that Brown said, "Don't kill me," but later admitted that he did not actually hear Brown or Wilson say anything. Wilson then fired two shots at "point blank range" from within two feet. The shots hit Brown in the face and Brown fell to the ground. Wilson then fired four or five shots into Brown's back after Brown was already dead, face first on the ground. Witness 128 then drove by Wilson and asked him why he shot Brown. Wilson told Witness 128 to "shut the fuck up," "mind [his] own business," and "keep going." Witness 128 then pulled into his complex and parked, staying away because he did not want to get shot himself. According to Witness 128, there were no other people or cars on the street, except for a white pick-up truck behind him.

Federal prosecutors and agents met with Witness 128 and challenged him on internal inconsistencies and statements he made that were inconsistent with physical evidence. Contrary to his previous account, he stated that when he pulled up on Canfield Drive, he saw Brown in the driver's side window of the SUV from his mid-chest up. He stated that Brown and Wilson were pulling on each other's shirts until Brown backed up. Wilson then held his gun out the window and fired a shot. As a result, Brown ran from the vehicle. Contrary to his previous statement to the FBI, Witness 128 told federal prosecutors that although he heard additional shots, he did not see them because he ducked down in his vehicle. For the first time, Witness 128 mentioned the presence of a female passenger in his vehicle. He could not identify the passenger, but explained that during the shooting, his attention was diverted to her because he was trying to keep her calm, as she had become hysterical.

Witness 128 explained that when he stopped ducking for cover, he saw Brown coming back toward Wilson with his hands up. Witness 128 stated that Wilson shot Brown, causing him to fall face down to the ground. He maintained that Wilson then stood over Brown and shot into his back. When federal prosecutors asked him to reconcile those final shots with the autopsy report that shows that Brown was not shot in the back, Witness 128 said he may have hallucinated but could not offer more of an explanation. He also admitted that much of what he initially said was assumption.

As mentioned, Witness 128 was one of two witnesses who identified his voice on the aforementioned video taken in the aftermath of the shooting depicting the two contractors. Witness 128 claimed to be the person off camera shouting, "He wasn't no threat at all," because he did not perceive Brown to be a threat. However, Witness 128 acknowledged that he did not know what happened at the SUV. Contrary to what he originally told the FBI, he did not see Brown run from the SUV, was mistaken about the final shots fired, and therefore did not know whether Brown was a threat to Wilson.

Witness 128 also admitted that he spoke to Brown's mother on the day of the shooting and shared details of the shooting. Witness 128 told Brown's mother that Wilson shot Brown at point blank range while his hands were up, and that even after Brown fell to his death, Wilson stood over Brown and fired several more times. Witness 128 also told several neighbors his inaccurate version of what happened, as they were gathering in the minutes and hours after the shooting. Several individuals identified Witness 128 through description as someone who was going around spreading a narrative that Brown was shot with his hands up in surrender.

Witness 128 has been convicted of multiple felonies including crimes of dishonesty, all of which would be admissible in federal court as impeachment evidence. Witness 128's accounts are inconsistent with each other, inconsistent with the forensic and physical evidence, and inconsistent with credible witness accounts. Accordingly, after a thorough review of the evidence, federal prosecutors determined this witness's accounts to lack credibility and therefore do not support a prosecution of Darren Wilson.

xxi.   **Witness 140**

Witness 140 is a 45-year-old white female who gave two statements to law enforcement and testified before the county grand jury. Witness 140 contacted SLCPD detectives in September 2014, claiming to have been a witness to the shooting of Brown, but too fearful to come forward when it happened. She explained that she decided it was time to come forward because she knew the case was being presented to the county grand jury and she was "tired of hearing that the officer is guilty." SLCPD and the FBI jointly interviewed Witness 140, who completely corroborated Wilson's account. Although the physical and forensic evidence was consistent with her account, the timing of her disclosure and the details of her narrative caused investigators to question her veracity. Therefore, federal prosecutors and agents conducted a follow-up interview.

During her follow-up interview, as in her initial account, Witness 140 claimed that she inadvertently ended up on Canfield Drive because she got lost on her way to visit a friend in Florissant, whom she had not seen in about 25 years. Witness 140 explained that she did not have a cell phone or a GPS, and was prone to getting lost. She pulled into the Canfield Green apartment complex to ask for directions, getting out of her car to do so. When federal prosecutors asked her why, as a woman, she would get out of her car in an unfamiliar neighborhood, she explained that she wanted to smoke a cigarette. Thereafter, while standing on the sidewalk, smoking a cigarette with a man from whom she was getting directions, she saw Wilson's SUV drive in the opposite direction of Brown and Witness 101, who were walking in the middle of the street. Witness 140 explained that she saw Wilson stop, speak to Brown and Witness 101, pull forward, and then back up. Wilson then tried to open the door of the SUV, but Brown punched it shut. Witness 101 grabbed the rearview mirror, bending it inward and catching his bracelet which broke and fell to the ground.

The specificity of this description initially caused SLCPD detectives concern because it mimicked an obscure media article which offered theories about how the SUV rearview mirror came to be folded inward and how beaded bracelets, found at the scene, landed on the ground. During Witness 140's follow-up interview, federal prosecutors asked her about this online article and Witness 140 acknowledged reading it prior to meeting with SLCPD detectives, possibly using it to fill in gaps in her memory.

According to Witness 140, she saw a struggle by the SUV, explaining that Brown was bent forward such that the top portion of his body, starting at the navel, was in the SUV. She described "childish wrestling" or "fist fighting" that ensued. She heard one gunshot from within the SUV, and then saw Brown run away, as Wilson shouted, "Stop. Freeze. I'm gonna shoot." Wilson fired a second gunshot as he got out of the SUV. Witness 140 described it as a possible "warning shot" because Brown did not "even flinch," indicating to her that he was not hit. Wilson then pursued Brown, who "made it further than where he got shot." Brown then turned around as Brown's arms flew upward, and Wilson stopped pursuing him. Brown bent forward in a "football-type" mode, hands balled up in fists, and "started charging." Witness 140 explained that Brown looked like "he was on something." Wilson looked panicked as he repeatedly shot Brown in the arm. Brown, however, kept coming at Wilson, who backed up as Brown closed the distance. Witness 140 heard a volley of four shots, a pause, and then two more shots before Brown fell to his death and "it got gross."

Witness 140 explained that she did not see Witness 101 after the initial interaction at the SUV until he reappeared five to 10 minutes after the shooting with his black t-shirt draped over his "wife-beater" tank top. This description matched how Witness 101 appeared in media interviews in the aftermath of the shooting. Also, seeing Witness 101 reappear conflicted with Witness 140's explanation that she immediately left Canfield Drive after the last shots because she was the only white woman in a neighborhood that was quickly growing hostile.

Investigators also questioned Witness 140 about the route she took out of the complex, which looks navigable on a map, but in reality is blocked by a concrete street barrier. Witness 140 responded that she is not good with directions, and was unsure the route she took. Since the shooting incident, she has acquired both a GPS and a mobile phone.

Witness 140 stated that she went immediately home and told no one about what she witnessed except her ex-husband. However, when SLCPD detectives attempted to verify this, Witness 140's ex-husband reported that Witness 140 has a tendency to lie. Witness 140's response was that her ex-husband was distrustful that the detectives were who they claimed to be. Nonetheless, Witness 140 acknowledged that she suffers from bouts of mania because she does not take her medicine for bipolar disorder and she suffered traumatic brain injury from a car crash several years ago.

Witness 140 also admitted to federal prosecutors that although she told no one about what she had witnessed, she posted comments on websites and Facebook about the shooting. Her comments were blatantly profane and racist. Furthermore, she was involved in developing a fundraising organization for first responders, and had a picture of a "thin blue line" as her Facebook profile picture.

During her testimony before the county grand jury, Witness 140 admitted that she did not get lost on Canfield Drive while en route to visit a high school friend, but rather she purposely went to Canfield Drive that day because she fears black people and was attempting to conquer her fears. However, in an effort to bolster he testimony, Witness 140 provided county prosecutors with a daily journal she claimed to keep, with one entry that documented the events of August 9. While that entry was detailed, all of the other entries were generic and sporadic.

Witness 140 was twice convicted of passing bad checks, felonies that are crimes of dishonesty and likely admissible in federal court as impeachment evidence. Although Witness 140's account of this incident is consistent with physical and forensic evidence and with credible witness accounts, large parts of her narrative have been admittedly fabricated from media accounts, and her bias in favor of Wilson is readily apparent. Accordingly, while her account likely is largely accurate, federal prosecutors determined that the account as a whole was not reliable and therefore did not consider it when making a prosecutive decision.

xxii. **Witness 139**

Witness 139 is 50-year-old black female. She made two statements, including her county grand jury testimony. As detailed below, Witness 139's initial account was riddled with inconsistencies from one sentence to the next. She was unable to provide a coherent narrative, and when she was asked to clarify, Witness 139 would respond with "you know what I mean," answer with a non sequitur, or break down in sobs. The details that she did provide were largely inconsistent with the physical evidence. Witness 139 was similarly incoherent and inconsistent when she testified before the county grand jury, unable to provide any sort of linear narrative.

Witness 139 reluctantly came to the NAACP office in St. Louis to meet with SLCPD detectives, FBI agents, and federal prosecutors. Through hysterical tears, she expressed fear in speaking with law enforcement because she felt pressured by the community to make a statement about what she had purportedly witnessed. She explained that ever since she gave a media interview,[25] people have been anonymously calling her. Witness 139 explained that these calls made her feel threatened, though she could not articulate how or why she felt threatened.

According to Witness 139, at about 2:30 to 3:00 p.m., she was driving eastbound on Canfield Drive, in the same direction she claimed Wilson's "four door car" was traveling, and the same direction in which Brown and Witness 101 were walking. She had difficulty distinguishing between Brown and Witness 101. Witness 139 stated that she was behind the police car, but pulled over to let him pass. Wilson then stopped his car to speak with Brown and Witness 101, though Witness 139 was inconsistent about whether two or three cars pulled past her and drove off or whether there were two or three cars in front of her when Wilson stopped. Witness 139 stated that Wilson told Brown and Witness 101 to use the sidewalk, but then said that she could not actually hear words. Rather, she just heard a deep voice. Either Brown or Witness 101 then walked toward the front of the police car and Wilson grabbed that person. Witness 139 could not be more descriptive, explaining that she had answered her mobile phone while this was happening.

Witness 139 explained that Wilson reached for his gun and held it straight out of the driver's side window, firing one or two shots. Later in her interview, she described Wilson holding the gun on the window frame when firing. Either way, Witness 139 explained that while this was happening, Witness 101 ran behind the police car. Brown was standing by the driver's side window, close enough to touch the car. However, she later described Brown being closer to the headlights of the car. When she saw those first gunshots, Witness 139 put her head down on the steering wheel, covering her eyes. Wilson then got out of his car, stood over Brown, and kept shooting. If Witness 139 was initially driving behind Wilson, she would have had the same vantage point as Witness 123 and Witness 133 in the white Monte Carlo, and therefore, would have been unable to see the driver's side of Wilson's vehicle and much of what she described.

Also inconsistent with what she initially described, Witness 139 said that Brown ran from the police car after the first two shots. She first claimed that Wilson shot Brown in the back as Brown was running, which caused Brown to turn around. Witness 139 also stated that Wilson was still getting out of his car when Brown turned around, making it unclear if Wilson shot at Brown as he was running away. To that end, Witness 139 also stated that she was not sure if the bullet struck him in the back. Regardless, Brown turned around, never moving forward from where he stood. According to Witness 139, Brown fell to the ground dead with his hands next to his head at right angles because his hands had been up. Wilson then fired at least three shots as Brown was lying face down on the ground. Witness 139 saw that Brown was bleeding from his back. When asked how she was able to witness the final shots if she had her head down in her arms, Witness 139 explained that she put her head down in her arms after the first two shots, but she could still see because she was peeking. Witness 139 claimed that when she asked Wilson if she could check on Brown because she is a nurse, he told her to "get the fuck on."

---

[25] There is no indication that Witness 139 ever gave a media interview that was broadcast to the public.

73

Witness 139 has no criminal history. Witness 139's account was incoherent and inconsistent throughout, markedly inconsistent with the physical and forensic evidence, and inconsistent with credible witness accounts. Wilson was driving an SUV westbound at noon, not a car eastbound at 2:30 p.m.; Wilson fired the first shot inside the SUV, not straight out the window; Brown moved toward Wilson and did not fall to his death where he turned around, nor did he die within an arm's length of the police vehicle; and Wilson did not stand over Brown and shoot him causing him to bleed from the back. Accordingly, federal prosecutors determined this witness's account not to be credible and therefore it does not support a prosecution of Darren Wilson.

xxiii. **Witness 120**

Witness 120 is a 19-year-old black male who said he was Brown's best friend and Witness 101's "cousin." Brown was staying with Witness 120 the night before the shooting occurred, during which time they did "a whole lot of talking about God" and "about the problems that [they have] been going through." Witness 120 explained that it seemed like Brown was "going through a phase."

Witness 120 gave three statements, including his testimony before the county grand jury. FBI agents and SCLPD detectives initially interviewed Witness 120 in the presence of his lawyer and his uncle. Witness 120 gave an internally inconsistent account that was also inconsistent with physical evidence. Federal prosecutors and agents interviewed Witness 120, with his lawyer present, in an attempt to determine what he actually witnessed.

According to Witness 120's initial account, he was on the phone on the third floor of his sister's apartment when he heard a gunshot. He instantly hopped up to look out the window because he knew that Brown and Witness 101 were walking to the store to get cigarillos to smoke marijuana later that day. When he looked out the window, Witness 120 saw Brown, who was facing the window, drop to his knees with his hands in the air, blood coming from his left shoulder and ribcage.[26] Brown's back was to the police vehicle. Witness 101 was next to Brown. Brown told Witness 101 to "run for your life." However, later in the same interview, Witness 120 stated that Witness 101 told him (Witness 120) that he, Witness 101, ran away after that first shot. When Witness 120 testified before the county grand jury, he said that he did not see Witness 101 until after the shooting was over.

According to Witness 120, Wilson then got out of the police cruiser, and positioned himself "a step away" from Brown, who stated, "Please don't shoot me." Wilson then shot Brown "point blank" in the head and Brown fell on his side. Wilson then fired eight more shots while Brown was on the ground, one of which grazed his arm.[27]

During his follow-up interview with federal prosecutors and federal agents, Witness 120 stated that he was asleep when Brown and Witness 101 left to go to the store. He woke to the sound of a gunshot. Witness 120 then repeated the same account as before: He went to the window and saw Brown on his knees with his hands up, situated about five feet from the police

---

[26] Autopsy results indicate that Brown was shot on his right side.

[27] Witness 120 cited to media reports as to why he knew that Brown was shot in the arm.

vehicle. Brown said, "Please don't shoot me," and Wilson fired a shot into Brown's head at "point blank" range. However, during the second interview, Witness 120 acknowledged that he never saw Wilson emerge from his vehicle and never saw any injury on Brown. Instead, he claimed that after that second shot, he ran downstairs and heard two volleys of four shots each with a pause in between. By the time he got downstairs, the gunfire had ended. Witness 120 explained that although he did not see the shots, common sense dictates that those eight shots struck Brown. He also explained that he based most of his recanted account on what people "in the community told [him]."

Although Witness 120 recanted most of his original statement, his version to federal prosecutors was still inconsistent with the autopsy results. Likewise, Witness 120 gave an inconsistent account to the county grand jury, admittedly based on rumor and hearsay, and motivated by his allegiance to his friend. When grand jurors questioned Witness 120 about inconsistencies with physical evidence, he dismissed the question, stating that Brown "was assassinated for what reason."

Witness 120's claim that Brown's body was found five feet from the police vehicle is inconsistent with the crime scene; Witness 120's description that Wilson shot Brown at point blank range is inconsistent with the autopsy results; Witness 120's description that he was at home at the time the first shots were fired is inconsistent with Witness 138's description that Witness 120 was at Witness 138's house when the shots were fired.

Witness 120 has a felony arrest that likely would be inadmissible in federal court as impeachment evidence. In addition to his accounts being riddled with inconsistencies with each other, the physical and forensic evidence, and credible witness accounts, Witness 120's account is driven by apparent bias for his friend. Accordingly, federal prosecutors determined his account to lack credibility and it does not therefore support a prosecution of Darren Wilson.

xxiv.   **Witness 148**

Witness 148 is a 26-year-old black female who did not report to federal authorities that she witnessed the shooting until late February, 2015. Witness 148 briefly spoke to federal prosecutors via telephone to provide a summary of what she witnessed on August 9, 2014. Based on that description, federal prosecutors and agents subsequently met with Witness 148 in person.

According to Witness 148, she was driving eastbound on Canfield Drive, traveling in the same direction as Brown and Witness 101. She drove past Wilson, who was driving his SUV, and Brown and Witness 101 who were walking in the street, but right next to the curb of the sidewalk. Contrary to all other evidence, they were not in the middle of the street. She heard Wilson say, "Get the fuck on the sidewalk," and she heard either Brown or Witness 101 respond that they were near their "destination." Suspecting something was going to happen between Wilson and Brown and Witness 101 because she is from Chicago and is used to bad interactions with police, she slowed down and watched over her right shoulder, out her back window. She heard tires "screech" and saw the SUV reverse back.

Witness 148 pulled her vehicle into a nearby parking lot and parked because she wanted to see what would happen next. She told her four-year-old son to wait in her car while she got out of her vehicle and watched as Brown and Wilson engaged in a struggle on the driver side of the SUV. Witness 148 stated her that her vantage point was of the passenger side of the SUV, but she could nonetheless see Brown using his hands to push off the driver's door as Wilson pulled Brown toward the SUV. She heard Brown repeatedly state, "I didn't do anything," as Wilson stated, "Stop resisting." Despite being in a parking lot and on the opposite side of the SUV as Brown, Witness 148 stated that Brown "looked scared and it's not like he's a giant or anything." Witness 148 also stated that Brown never put his hands inside the SUV window, despite forensic and physical evidence to the contrary. However, she ultimately acknowledged to prosecutors that because she could not see the driver's side of the SUV, she did not know whether Brown put his hands inside the SUV window.

According to Witness 148, her son then got out of her vehicle because he wanted to watch what was happening. Witness 148 heard a gunshot. Witness 148 got down on the grass and covered her child's body with her own to protect him. While doing so, she watched Witness 101 and then Brown run from the SUV. After that, Witness 101 disappeared and she never saw him again. Wilson then emerged from the SUV and fired at least two shots. Brown flinched, arching his body back as though the bullet had "grazed" him. Brown then turned around and put his hands up in right angles at shoulder-height in a sign of surrender. He then dropped to his knees, and started to say something like, "I don't have a -," but was cut off as Wilson walked toward Brown firing at least six shots, killing Brown. Witness 148 described Wilson as "possessed" based on the "look in his eyes," as though "he wasn't human." It is unclear based on Witness 148's description how she was able to see both the look in Wilson's eyes and Brown trying to speak as he was surrendering, all at the same time.

Witness 148 was initially adamant that, contrary to DNA evidence in the roadway and credible witness accounts that establish otherwise, Brown never moved forward from the spot where he turned around to face Wilson. When prosecutors specifically asked her about this, Witness 148 acknowledged that because he son was squirming on the ground and she feared for his safety, her attention may have been diverted during the shooting, and therefore she may have missed parts of it. Nonetheless, she repeated that Wilson shot Brown as he was "surrendering."

When prosecutors and agents pressed Witness 148 as to why it took her nearly seven months to come forward and report what she witnessed, she explained that she feared the FPD. She maintained that she did not tell anyone – "not one living soul" – about what she witnessed on August 9, 2014. Witness 148 stated however, that she was she was not going to live in fear and therefore went to Ferguson every day since the shooting until the day of the county grand jury's decision on November 24, 2014. She protested and marched, but never shared with anyone what she witnessed, including her god-daughter who started a "Michael Brown movement." However, Witness 148 met a close friend of the Brown family after a Martin Luther King Day protest. Several weeks after that, she told the friend what she had witnessed and ultimately met with Brown's mother. Witness 148 explained that as a mother herself, she wanted to share with Brown's mother what happened to Brown.

Federal prosecutors asked Witness 148 why she chose not report to the FBI or the SLCPD, since her distrust was specific to the FPD. Witness 148 explained that she did not know that either of those agencies was investigating, despite the fact that she went to Ferguson everyday for three months and admittedly, read media reports about the shooting in the hours, days, and weeks after it occurred.

Witness 148 has felony convictions including conviction for a crime of dishonesty that would be admissible in federal court as impeachment evidence. Her account is inconsistent with the physical and forensic evidence, inconsistent with undisputed facts, *i.e.* Brown and Witness 101 were in fact walking in the middle of the street, and she admittedly did not see portions of the incident based on her vantage point and because she was protecting her child from gunfire. Similar to Witness 140, even if Witness 148 was present on Canfield Drive on August 14, 2014, and saw parts of the incident, Witness 148's account is inherently unreliable and subject to extensive cross-examination based on how she obtained her information and what motivated her to come forward. She did not report what she witnessed for nearly seven months without any reasonable explanation for the delay, giving her ample opportunity to research the facts in the form of media stories and county grand jury transcripts; she has an apparent distrust of the police (she told federal prosecutors at the outset of her interview that she "didn't trust police at all"); she is upset that "Darren Wilson got away" with what she believes to be a crime and then subsequently engaged in months of protests, but yet she failed to report it to the FBI, not because of distrust, but because she was unaware of the federal investigation. This is difficult to reconcile in light of both her daily visits to Ferguson while the FBI was canvassing the area and her regular internet searches about the shooting. For these reasons, federal prosecutors did not credit her account and could not rely upon it to support a prosecution of Darren Wilson.

xxv.   Other Individuals Who Did Not Witness the Shootings

Throughout the course of the two investigations, FBI agents and SLCPD detectives both jointly and independently monitored social media, print media, and local and national television broadcasts and news reports in an effort to locate potential witnesses and sources of information. Investigators tracked down several individuals who, via the aforementioned media, claimed to have witnessed Wilson shooting Brown as Brown held his hands up in clear surrender. All of these purported witnesses, upon being interviewed by law enforcement, acknowledged that they did not actually witness the shooting, but rather repeated what others told them in the immediate aftermath of the shooting.

For example, one individual publicly posted a description of the shooting during a Facebook chat, explaining that Brown "threw his hands up in the air" as Wilson shot him dead. A Twitter user took a screenshot of the description and "tweeted" it throughout the social media site. When the SLCPD and the FBI interviewed the individual who made the initial post, he explained that he "gave a brief description of what [he] was hearing from the people that were outside" on Canfield Drive, but he did not witness the incident itself. Similarly, another individual publicly "tweeted" about the shooting as though he had just witnessed it, even though he had not.

Likewise, another individual appeared on a television program and discussed the shooting as if he had seen it firsthand. When law enforcement interviewed him, he explained that it was a "misconception" that he witnessed the shooting. He spoke to the host of the show because he was asked if he wanted to talk about the shooting. In so doing, he was inaccurately portrayed as a witness.

Another individual recorded the aforementioned video of the contractors taken in the aftermath of the shootings. When an FBI agent and federal prosecutor met with that individual, he explained that because the video had been widely circulated in the media, many people incorrectly believed that he had witnessed the shooting. He did not witness the shootings, and was initially unsurprised to hear gunshots because it was not uncommon to hear gunfire in the neighborhood. He started recording after the gunshots abated by placing his iPad in the ground-level window of his basement apartment. He provided federal authorities with that video and other videos taken minutes after the shooting. Several videos captured conversations of bystanders on Canfield Drive, standing by police tape as paramedics covered Brown's body with two more sheets in addition to the one that was already covering him. During those conversations, bystanders discussed what transpired, although none of what was recorded was consistent with the physical evidence or credible accounts from other witnesses. For example, one woman stated that the officer shot at Brown from inside his vehicle while the SUV was still moving and then the "officer stood over [Brown] and pow-pow-pow."

Because none of these individuals actually witnessed the shooting incident and admitted so to law enforcement, federal prosecutors did not consider their inaccurate postings, tweets, media interviews, and the like when making a prosecutive decision.

IV. **Legal Analysis**

The evidence discussed above does not meet the standards for presentation of an indictment set forth in the USAM and in the governing federal law. The evidence is insufficient to establish probable cause or to prove beyond a reasonable doubt a violation of 18 U.S.C. § 242 and would not be likely to survive a defense motion for acquittal at trial pursuant to Federal Rule of Criminal Procedure 29(a). This is true for all six to eight shots that struck Brown. Witness accounts suggesting that Brown was standing still with his hands raised in an unambiguous signal of surrender when Wilson shot Brown are inconsistent with the physical evidence, are otherwise not credible because of internal inconsistencies, or are not credible because of inconsistencies with other credible evidence. In contrast, Wilson's account of Brown's actions, if true, would establish that the shootings were not objectively unreasonable under the relevant Constitutional standards governing an officer's use of deadly force. Multiple credible witnesses corroborate virtually every material aspect of Wilson's account and are consistent with the physical evidence. Even if the evidence established that Wilson's actions were unreasonable, the government would also have to prove that Wilson acted willfully, *i.e.* that he acted with a specific intent to violate the law. As discussed above, Wilson's stated intent for shooting Brown was in response to a perceived deadly threat. The only possible basis for prosecuting Wilson under Section 242 would therefore be if the government could prove that his account is not true – *i.e.*, that Brown never punched and grabbed Wilson at the SUV, never struggled with Wilson over the gun, and thereafter clearly surrendered in a way that no reasonable officer could have failed to perceive. Not only do eyewitnesses and physical evidence corroborate Wilson's account, but there is no credible evidence to disprove Wilson's perception that Brown posed a threat to Wilson as Brown advanced toward him. Accordingly, seeking his indictment is not permitted by Department of Justice policy or the governing law.

A.   <u>Legal Standard</u>

To obtain a conviction of Darren Wilson at trial for his actions in shooting Michael Brown, the government must prove the following elements beyond a reasonable doubt: (1) that Wilson was acting under color of law; (2) that he acted willfully; (3) that he deprived Brown of a right protected by the Constitution or laws of the United States; and (4) that the deprivation resulted in bodily injury or death. The Constitutional right at stake depends on Brown's custodial status at the time Wilson shot him. *See Graham*, 490 U.S. at 395; *Loch v. City of Litchfield*, 689 F.3d 961, 965 (8th Cir. 2012). In this case, Wilson had attempted to stop and possibly arrest Brown. The rights of an arrestee are governed by the Fourth Amendment's prohibition against unreasonable searches and seizures, which includes the right to be free from excessive force during the course of an arrest. *See Nelson v. County of Wright*, 162 F.3d 986, 990 (8th Cir. 1998). Under the Fourth Amendment, an officer's use of force must be "objectively reasonable" under the facts and circumstances known to the officer at the time he made the decision to use physical force. *Id.* Establishing that the intent behind a Constitutional violation is "willful" requires proof that the officer acted with the purpose "to deprive a person of a right which has been made specific either by the express terms of the Constitution or laws of the United States or by decisions interpreting them." *See United States v. Lanier*, 520 U.S. 259, 267 (1997), *citing Screws v. United States*, 325 U.S. 91 (1945). While the officer need not be "thinking in Constitutional terms" when deciding to use force, he must know what he is doing is wrong and decide to do it anyway. *Screws* at 106-07. Mistake, panic, misperception, or even poor judgment by a police officer does not provide a basis for prosecution under Section 242. *See United States v. McClean*, 528 F.2d 1250, 1255 (2d Cir. 1976) (inadvertence or mistake negates willfulness for purposes of 18 U.S.C. § 242).

There is no dispute that Wilson, who was on duty and working as a patrol officer for the FPD, acted under color of law when he shot Brown, or that the shots resulted in Brown's death. The determination of whether criminal prosecution is appropriate rests on whether there is sufficient evidence to establish that any of the shots fired by Wilson were unreasonable given the facts known to Wilson at the time, and if so, whether Wilson fired the shots with the requisite "willful" criminal intent, which, in this case, would require proof that Wilson shot Brown under conditions that no reasonable officer could have perceived as a threat.

B. <u>Uses of Force</u>

Under the Fourth Amendment, a police officer's use of physical force against an arrestee must be objectively reasonable under the circumstances. *Graham*, 490 U.S. at 396-97 (1989). "The 'reasonableness' of a particular use of force must be judged from the perspective of a reasonable officer on the scene, rather than with the 20/20 vision of hindsight." *Id.* at 396. "Careful attention" must be paid "to the facts and circumstances of each particular case, including the severity of the crime at issue, whether the suspect poses an immediate threat to the safety of the officers or others, and whether he is actively resisting arrest or attempting to evade arrest by flight." *Id.* Allowance must be made for the fact that law enforcement officials are often forced to make split-second judgments in circumstances that are tense, uncertain, and rapidly evolving. *Id.* at 396-97.

The use of deadly force is justified when the officer has "probable cause to believe that the suspect pose[s] a threat of serious physical harm, either to the officer or to others." *Tennessee v. Garner*, 471 U.S. 1, 11 (1985); *see Nelson*, 162 F.3d at 990; *O'Bert ex. rel. Estate of O'Bert v. Vargo*, 331 F.3d 29, 36 (2d Cir. 2003) (same as *Garner*); *Deluna v. City of Rockford*, 447 F.3d 1008, 1010 (7th Cir. 2006), *citing Scott v. Edinburg*, 346 F.3d 752, 756 (7th Cir. 2003) (deadly force can be reasonably employed where an officer believes that the suspect's actions place him, or others in the immediate vicinity, in imminent danger of death or serious bodily injury). An officer may use deadly force under certain circumstances even if the suspect is fleeing. "Where the officer has probable cause to believe that the suspect poses a threat of serious physical harm, either to the officer or to others, it is not constitutionally unreasonable to prevent escape by using deadly force. Thus, if the suspect threatens the officer with a weapon or there is probable cause to believe that he has committed a crime involving the infliction or threatened infliction of serious physical harm, deadly force may be used if necessary to prevent escape, and if, where feasible, some warning has been given." *See Garner*, 471 U.S. at 11-12.

An officer may not, on the other hand, use physical force, deadly or otherwise, once a threat has been neutralized. This is true even if the suspect threatened an officer's life – or that of another – prior to being brought under control. *See Moore v. Indehar*, 514 F.3d 756, 762 (8th Cir. 2008); *Nelson*, 162 F.3d at 990. For that reason, every instance in which Wilson shot Brown could potentially be prosecuted if the deployment of deadly force was objectively unreasonable in the particular circumstance. We must therefore determine whether, each time he fired his weapon, the available evidence could prove that Wilson acted reasonably or unreasonably in light of the facts available to him at the time. In particular, we must examine whether the available evidence shows that Wilson reasonably believed that Brown posed a threat of serious bodily harm to Wilson himself or others in the community, or whether Brown clearly attempted to surrender, prior to any of the shots fired by Wilson.

1. Shooting at the SUV

The evidence establishes that the shots fired by Wilson while he was seated in his SUV were in self-defense and thus were not objectively unreasonable under the Fourth Amendment. According to Wilson, when he backed up his SUV and attempted to get out to speak with Brown, Brown blocked him from opening the door. Brown then reached through the window and began to punch Wilson in the face, after which he reached for and gained control of Wilson's firearm by putting his hand over Wilson's hand. As Brown was struggling for the gun and pointing it into Wilson's hip, Wilson gained control of the firearm and fired it just over his lap at Brown's hand. The physical evidence corroborates Wilson's account in that the bullet was recovered from the door panel just over Wilson's lap, the base of Brown's hand displayed injuries consistent with it being within inches of the muzzle of the gun, and Wilson had injuries to his jaw consistent with being struck. Witnesses 102, 103, and 104 all state that they saw Brown with the upper portion of his body and/or arms inside the SUV as he struggled with Wilson. These witnesses have given consistent statements, and their statements are also consistent with the physical evidence.

In contrast, the two primary witnesses who state that Wilson instigated the encounter by grabbing Brown and pulling him toward the SUV and that Brown's hands were never inside the vehicle are Witnesses 101 and 127. Both of those witnesses have given accounts that are inconsistent with the forensic and physical evidence. For example, both witnesses insisted that Wilson shot Brown in the back as he fled and that they saw shots hit Brown in the back. These statements are contradicted by all three autopsies, which concluded that Brown had no entry wounds to his back. Both witnesses also insist that, after he turned to face Wilson, Brown raised his hands, never moved forward, and never reached for his waistband. While Brown might well have briefly raised his hands in some fashion (see below), the physical evidence in the form of the blood on the ground establishes that he did move forward and that he fell to the ground with his left hand near his waistband. Both of these accounts are further undermined by the witnesses' physical inability to perceive what they claim to have seen. Witness 101 was hiding behind a vehicle for significant portions of the incident and Witness 127 was looking at her cell phone, attempting to make a video recording of the encounter, and driving her car. Given the deficiencies in the accounts of these two witnesses, federal prosecutors credited the accounts of Witnesses 102, 103, 104, and Wilson and concluded that Brown did in fact reach for and attempt to grab Wilson's gun, that Brown could have overpowered Wilson, which was acknowledged even by Witness 101, and that Wilson fired his weapon just over his own lap in an attempt to regain control of a dangerous situation.

Under well-established Fourth Amendment precedent, it is not objectively unreasonable for a law enforcement officer to use deadly force in response to being physically assaulted by a subject who attempts to take his firearm. *See, e.g., Nelson*, 162 F.3d at 990-91 (holding that it was not objectively unreasonable for officer to shoot at a suspect through a closet door after suspect attempted to grab his gun, hit him in the head with an asp, and pushed him into closet). The government therefore cannot meet its burden of establishing probable cause to a grand jury or proving beyond a reasonable doubt to twelve trial jurors that the shots fired by Wilson at the SUV were unreasonable. These shots are thus not prosecutable violations of 18 U.S.C. § 242.

2. Wilson's Subsequent Pursuit of Brown and Shots Allegedly Fired as Brown Was Running Away

The evidence does not support concluding that Wilson shot Brown while Brown's back was toward Wilson. Witnesses, such as Witness 118, Witness 128, Witness 139 and others, who claim to have seen Wilson fire directly into Brown's back, gave accounts that lack credibility because the physical evidence establishes that there were no entry wounds to Brown's back, although there was a wound to the anatomical back of Brown's right arm, and a graze wound to Brown's right arm. Also, other witnesses who say that Wilson fired at Brown as he ran have given accounts that are not credible because significant aspects of their statements are irreconcilable with the physical evidence, such as Witness 101 and 127, whose statements are suspect for the reasons noted above. Similarly, Witness 124 claims to have seen Wilson following behind Brown while steadily firing at him. However, Witness 124 dramatically changed her accounts of what she saw between the time of her first statement to the SLCPD and second statement to the FBI. She refused to meet with the federal prosecutors to clarify her varying accounts. Also, her account was dramatically different from that of her husband, Witness 115, who was standing next to her during the incident. Witness 115 stated that he thought he saw Wilson fire once at Brown as he was running away, but other aspects of his account lack credibility for the reasons set forth above, *i.e.* he did not witness significant parts of the shooting and based parts of his account on assumption. Witnesses 128 and 137 initially claimed that Wilson fired at Brown while he was running away, but then acknowledged that they did not see what Wilson and Brown were doing at this point and thus do not know whether Wilson fired at Brown as he was running away. Witnesses 105 and 106 thought they saw Wilson fire at Brown as he was running, but describe seeing Brown hit in the leg and back in a manner that does not match the autopsy findings. Accordingly, there is no credible evidence that establishes that Wilson fired at or struck Brown's back as Brown fled.

3. Shots Fired After Brown Turned to Face Wilson

The evidence establishes that the shots fired by Wilson after Brown turned around were in self-defense and thus were not objectively unreasonable under the Fourth Amendment. The physical evidence establishes that after he ran about 180 feet away from the SUV, Brown turned and faced Wilson, then moved toward Wilson until Wilson finally shot him in the head and killed him. According to Wilson, Brown balled or clenched his fists and "charged" forward, ignoring commands to stop. Knowing that Brown was much larger than him and that he had previously attempted to overpower him and take his gun, Wilson stated that he feared for his safety and fired at Brown. Again, even Witness 101's account supports this perception. Brown then reached toward his waistband, causing Wilson to fear that Brown was reaching for a weapon. Wilson stated that he continued to fear for his safety at this point and fired at Brown again. Wilson finally shot Brown in the head as he was falling or lunging forward, after which Brown immediately fell to the ground. Wilson did not fire any additional shots. Wilson's version of events is corroborated by the physical evidence that indicates that Brown moved forward toward Wilson after he ran from the SUV, by the fact that Brown went to the ground with his left hand at (although not inside) his waistband, and by credible eyewitness accounts.

Wilson's version is further supported by disinterested eyewitnesses Witness 102, Witness 104, Witness 105, Witness 108, and Witness 109, among others. These witnesses all agree that Brown ran or charged toward Wilson and that Wilson shot at Brown only as Brown moved toward him. Although some of the witnesses stated that Brown briefly had his hands up or out at about waist-level, none of these witnesses perceived Brown to be attempting to surrender at any point when Wilson fired upon him. To the contrary, several of these witnesses stated that they would have felt threatened by Brown and would have responded in the same way Wilson did. For example, Witness 104 stated that as Wilson ran after Brown yelling "stop, stop, stop," Brown finally turned around and raised his hands "for a second." However, Brown then immediately balled his hands into fists and "charged" at Wilson in a "tackle run." Witness 104 stated that Wilson fired only when Brown moved toward him and that she "would have fired sooner." Likewise, Witness 105 stated that Brown turned around and put his hands up "for a brief moment," then refused a command from Wilson to "get down" and instead put his hands "in running position" and started running toward Wilson. Witness 105 stated that Wilson shot at Brown only when Brown was moving toward him. These witnesses' accounts are consistent with prior statements they have given, consistent with the forensic and physical evidence, and consistent with each other's accounts. Accordingly, we conclude that these accounts are credible.

Furthermore, there are no witnesses who could testify credibly that Wilson shot Brown while Brown was clearly attempting to surrender. The accounts of the witnesses who have claimed that Brown raised his hands above his head to surrender and said "I don't have a gun," or "okay, okay, okay" are inconsistent with the physical evidence or can be challenged in other material ways, and thus cannot be relied upon to form the foundation of a federal prosecution.[28] The two most prominent witnesses who have stated that Brown was shot with his hands up in surrender are Witness 101 and Witness 127, both of whom claim that Brown turned around with his hands raised in surrender, that he never reached for his waistband, that he never moved forward toward Wilson after turning to face him with his hands up, and that he fell to the ground with his hands raised. These and other aspects of their statements are contradicted by the physical evidence. Crime scene photographs establish that Brown fell to the ground with his left hand at his waistband and his right hand at his side. Brown's blood in the roadway demonstrates that Brown came forward at least 21.6 feet from the time he turned around toward Wilson. Other aspects of the accounts of Witness 101 and Witness 127 would render them not credible in a prosecution of Wilson, namely their accounts of what happened at the SUV. Both claim that Wilson fired the first shot out the SUV window, Witness 101 claims that the shot hit Brown at close range in the torso, and both claim that Brown did not reach inside the vehicle. These claims are irreconcilable with the bullet in the SUV door, the close-range wound to Brown's hand, Brown's DNA inside Wilson's car and on his gun, and the injuries to Wilson's face.

Other witnesses who have suggested that Brown was shot with his hands up in surrender have either recanted their statements, such as Witnesses 119 and 125, provided inconsistent statements, such as Witness 124, or have provided accounts that are verifiably untrue, such as Witnesses 121, 139, and 132. Witness 122 recanted significant portions of his statement by acknowledging that he was not in a position to see what either Brown or Wilson were doing, and who falsely insisted that three police officers pursued Brown and that the shooter was heavy set (in contrast to the slimly-built Wilson). Similar to Witness 128, Witness 122 told Brown's family that Brown had been shot execution-style. Witness 120 initially told law enforcement that he saw Brown shot at point-blank range as he was on his knees with his hands up. Similar to Witness 138, Witness 120 subsequently acknowledged that he did not see Brown get shot but "assumed" he had been executed while on his knees with his hands up based on "common sense" and what others "in the community told [him.]" There is no witness who has stated that Brown had his hands up in surrender whose statement is otherwise consistent with the physical evidence. For example, some witnesses say that Wilson only fired his weapon out of the SUV, (e.g. Witnesses 128, 101, and 127) or that Wilson stood next to the SUV and killed Brown right there (e.g. Witnesses 139, 132, 120). Some witnesses insist that Wilson shot Brown in the back as he lay on the ground. (e.g. Witnesses 128 and 139). Some witnesses say that Wilson shot Brown and he went to the ground immediately upon turning to face Wilson. (e.g. Witnesses 138, 101, 118, and 127). Some say Wilson went to the ground with his hands raised at right angles. (e.g. Witnesses 138, 118, and 121). Again, all of these statements are contradicted by the physical and forensic evidence, which also undermines the credibility of their accounts of other aspects of the incident, including their assertion that Brown had his hands up in a surrender position when Wilson shot him.

---

[28] The media has widely reported that there is witness testimony that Brown said "don't shoot" as he held his hands above his head. In fact, our investigation did not reveal any eyewitness who stated that Brown said "don't shoot."

When the shootings are viewed, as they must be, in light of all the surrounding circumstances and what Wilson knew at the time, as established by the credible physical evidence and eyewitness testimony, it was not unreasonable for Wilson to fire on Brown until he stopped moving forward and was clearly subdued. Although, with hindsight, we know that Brown was not armed with a gun or other weapon, this fact does not render Wilson's use of deadly force objectively unreasonable. Again, the key question is whether Brown could reasonably have been perceived to pose a deadly threat to Wilson at the time he shot him regardless of whether Brown was armed. Sufficient credible evidence supports Wilson's claim that he reasonably perceived Brown to be posing a deadly threat. First, Wilson did not know that Brown was not armed at the time he shot him, and had reason to suspect that he might be when Brown reached into the waistband of his pants as he advanced toward Wilson. *See Loch v. City of Litchfield*, 689 F.3d 961, 966 (8th Cir. 2012) (holding that "[e]ven if a suspect is ultimately 'found to be unarmed, a police officer can still employ deadly force if objectively reasonable.'") (quoting *Billingsley v. City of Omaha*, 277 F.3d 990, 995 (8th Cir. 2002)); *Reese v. Anderson*, 926 F.2d 494, 501 (5th Cir. 1991) ("Also irrelevant is the fact that [the suspect] was actually unarmed. [The officer] did not and could not have known this."); *Smith v. Freland*, 954 F.2d 343, 347 (noting that "unarmed" does not mean "harmless) (6th Cir. 1992). While Brown did not use a gun on Wilson at the SUV, his aggressive actions would have given Wilson reason to at least question whether he might be armed, as would his subsequent forward advance and reach toward his waistband. This is especially so in light of the rapidly-evolving nature of the incident. Wilson did not have time to determine whether Brown had a gun and was not required to risk being shot himself in order to make a more definitive assessment.

Moreover, Wilson could present evidence that a jury likely would credit that he reasonably perceived a deadly threat from Brown even if Brown's hands were empty and he had never reached into his waistband because of Brown's actions in refusing to halt his forward movement toward Wilson. The Eighth Circuit Court of Appeals' decision in *Loch v. City of Litchfield* is dispositive on this point. There, an officer shot a suspect eight times as he advanced toward the officer. Although the suspect's "arms were raised above his head or extended at his sides," the Court of Appeals held that a reasonable officer could have perceived the suspect's forward advance in the face of the officer's commands to stop as resistance and a threat. As the Court of Appeals explained:

> Although [the suspect] had by this time thrown his firearm in the snow, … [the officer] did not observe that action. Instead of complying with [the officer's] command to get on the ground, [the suspect] turned and moved toward the officer. [Plaintiffs], noting that [the suspect's] arms were raised above his head or extended at his sides, suggest that [the suspect] was simply trying to find a suitable place to get on the ground, because his truck sat near a tree and snowbank. But even if [the suspect's] motives were innocent, a reasonable officer on the scene could have interpreted [the suspect's] actions as resistance. *It is undisputed that [the suspect] continued toward [the officer] despite the officer's repeated orders to get on the ground …. Thus, a reasonable officer could believe that [the suspect's] failure to comply was a matter of choice rather than necessity.*

Loch, 689 F.3d 961, 966 (8th Cir. 2012) (emphasis added).

Were the government to prosecute Wilson, the court would instruct the jury using *Loch* as a foundation. Given the evidence in this matter, jurors would likely conclude that Wilson had reason to be concerned that Brown was a threat to him as he continued to advance, just as did the officer in *Loch*.

In addition, even assuming that Wilson definitively knew that Brown was not armed, Wilson was aware that Brown had already assaulted him once and attempted to gain control of his gun. Wilson could thus present evidence that he reasonably feared that, if left unimpeded, Brown would again assault Wilson, again attempt to overpower him, and again attempt to take his gun. Under the law, Wilson has a strong argument that he was justified in firing his weapon at Brown as he continued to advance toward him and refuse commands to stop, and the law does not require Wilson to wait until Brown was close enough to physically assault Wilson. Even if, with hindsight, Wilson could have done something other than shoot Brown, the Fourth Amendment does not second-guess a law enforcement officer's decision on how to respond to an advancing threat. The law gives great deference to officers for their necessarily split-second judgments, especially in incidents such as this one that unfold over a span of less than two minutes. "Thus, under *Graham*, we must avoid substituting our personal notions of proper police procedure for the instantaneous decision of the officer at the scene. We must never allow the theoretical, sanitized world of our imagination to replace the dangerous and complex world that policemen face every day." *Smith*, 954 F.2d at 347 (6th Cir. 1992). *See also Ryburn v. Huff*, 132 S. Ct. 987, 991-92 (2012) (courts "should be cautious about second-guessing a police officer's assessment, made on the scene, of the danger presented by a particular situation"); *Estate of Morgan v. Cook*, 686 F.3d 494, 497 (8th Cir. 2012) ("The Constitution ... requires only that the seizure be objectively reasonable, not that the officer pursue the most prudent course of conduct as judged by 20/20 hindsight vision." (citing *Cole v. Bone*, 993 F.2d 1328, 1334 (8th Cir. 1993)) "It may appear, in the calm aftermath, that an officer could have taken a different course, but we do not hold the police to such a demanding standard." (citing *Gardner v. Buerger*, 82 F.3d 248, 251 (8th Cir. 1996) (same))). Rather, where, as here, an officer points his gun at a suspect to halt his advance, that suspect should be on notice that "escalation of the situation would result in the use of the firearm." *Estate of Morgan* at 498. An officer is permitted to continue firing until the threat is neutralized. *See Plumhoff v. Rickard*, 134 S.Ct. 2012, 2022 (2014) ("Officers need not stop shooting until the threat has ended").

For all of the reasons stated, Wilson's conduct in shooting Brown as he advanced on Wilson, and until he fell to the ground, was not objectively unreasonable and thus not a violation of 18 U.S.C. § 242.

C. **Willfulness**

Even if federal prosecutors determined there were sufficient evidence to convince twelve jurors beyond a reasonable doubt that Wilson used unreasonable force, federal law requires that the government must also prove that the officer acted willfully, that is, with the purpose to violate the law. *Screws v. United States*, 325 U.S. 91, 101-107 (1945) (discussing willfulness element of 18 U.S.C. § 242). The Supreme Court has held that an act is done willfully if it was "committed" either "in open defiance or in reckless disregard of a constitutional requirement which has been made specific and definite." *Screws*, 325 U.S. at 105. The government need not show that the defendant knew a federal statute or law protected the right with which he intended to interfere. *Id.* at 106-07 ("[t]he fact that the defendants may not have been thinking in constitutional terms is not material where their aim was not to enforce local law but to deprive a citizen of a right and that right was protected"); *United States v. Walsh*, 194 F.3d 37, 52-53 (2d Cir. 1999) (holding that jury did not have to find defendant knew of the particular Constitutional provision at issue but that it had to find intent to invade interest protected by Constitution). However, we must prove that the defendant intended to engage in the conduct that violated the Constitution and that he did so knowing that it was a wrongful act. *Id.*

"[A]ll the attendant circumstance[s]" should be considered in determining whether an act was done willfully. *Screws*, 325 U.S. at 107. Evidence regarding the egregiousness of the conduct, its character and duration, the weapons employed and the provocation, if any, is therefore relevant to this inquiry. *Id.* Willfulness may be inferred from blatantly wrongful conduct. *See id.* at 106; *see also United States v. Reese*, 2 F.3d 870, 881 (9th Cir. 1993) ("Intentionally wrongful conduct, because it contravenes a right definitely established in law, evidences a reckless disregard for that right; such reckless disregard, in turn, is the legal equivalent of willfulness."); *United States v. Dise*, 763 F.2d 586, 592 (3d Cir. 1985) (holding that when defendant invades personal liberty of another, knowing that invasion is violation of state law, defendant has demonstrated bad faith and reckless disregard for federal constitutional rights). Mistake, fear, misperception, or even poor judgment do not constitute willful conduct prosecutable under the statute. *See United States v. McClean*, 528 F.2d 1250, 1255 (2d Cir. 1976) (inadvertence or mistake negates willfulness for purposes of 18 U.S.C. § 242).

As discussed above, Darren Wilson has stated his intent in shooting Michael Brown was in response to a perceived deadly threat. The only possible basis for prosecuting Wilson under section 242 would therefore be if the government could prove that his account is not true – *i.e.*, that Brown never assaulted Wilson at the SUV, never attempted to gain control of Wilson's gun, and thereafter clearly surrendered in a way that no reasonable officer could have failed to perceive. Given that Wilson's account is corroborated by physical evidence and that his perception of a threat posed by Brown is corroborated by other eyewitnesses, to include aspects of the testimony of Witness 101, there is no credible evidence that Wilson willfully shot Brown as he was attempting to surrender or was otherwise not posing a threat. Even if Wilson was mistaken in his interpretation of Brown's conduct, the fact that others interpreted that conduct the same way as Wilson precludes a determination that he acted with a bad purpose to disobey the law. The same is true even if Wilson could be said to have acted with poor judgment in the manner in which he first interacted with Brown, or in pursuing Brown after the incident at the SUV. These are matters of policy and procedure that do not rise to the level of a Constitutional violation and thus cannot support a criminal prosecution. *Cf. Gardner v. Howard*, 109 F.3d 427, 430–31 (8th Cir. 1997) (violation of internal policies and procedures does not in and of itself rise to violation of Constitution).

Because Wilson did not act with the requisite criminal intent, it cannot be proven beyond reasonable doubt to a jury that he violated 18 U.S.C.§ 242 when he fired his weapon at Brown.

VI. Conclusion

For the reasons set forth above, this matter lacks prosecutive merit and should be closed.